Whatnots & Curios

A Selection of Articles and Reviews by Storm Constantine

Whatnots and Curios

A Selection of Articles and Reviews

Storm Constantine

IMMANION PRESS

Stafford England

Whatnots and Curios: A Selection of Articles and Reviews
By Storm Constantine
© 2015

http://www.stormconstantine.co.uk

ISBN 978-1-907737-69-5

IP0044

Cover art and design by Danielle Lainton
Interior layout by Storm Constantine
Thanks to Paula Wakefield for copy-editing

Set in Palatino Linotype

An Immanion Press Edition
http://www.immanion-press.com
info@immanion-press.com

Books by Storm Constantine

Short Story Collections:
*The Thorn Boy and Other Dreams of Dark Desire
*Mythangelus
*Mythophidia
*Mytholumina
*Mythanimus

Wraeththu Mythos Collections
(co-edited with Wendy Darling, including stories by the editors and other writers)
*ParaGenesis
*Para Imminence
*Para Kindred

Non-Fiction
*Sekhem Heka
*Grimoire Dehara: Kaimana
The Inward Revolution (with Deborah Benstead)
Egyptian Birth Signs (with Graham Phillips)
Bast and Sekhmet: Eyes of Ra (with Eloise Coquio)

*available as Immanion Press editions

Contents

Introductions

Myth, Magic and Healing

Introduction

Over the years, I've written hundreds of articles, reviews and essays – many of which, especially the smaller pieces, have vanished. However, I still have a lot of them and decided to publish a selection in book form. To me, it's interesting to see how my views have changed over the years; intrinsically similar, perhaps, but less heated.

The trouble with having decades of a writing career is that so much material has been lost or forgotten – usually small articles I was asked to produce quickly and which were never transferred from ancient computer disks to more current media storage. But some pieces from my earlier writing period have survived and are presented here as 'snapshots' of my history.

The book is divided into five sections: 'Reviews', 'On My Own Work', 'On the Craft of Writing', 'Introductions' and 'Myth, Magic and Healing'.

I've written a great many reviews of books, films and games over the years, but for this volume I selected a mix of reviews of books I'd disliked and loved. There is also an appraisal of the film 'Alexander' by Oliver Stone. The video game reviews, of which there were a lot, I thought too specialised an interest for a book of this type. Also, games date far more quickly than books or films, so are mostly irrelevant now.

In the section concerning my own work you'll find one in which I more or less state I'll never write another Wraeththu story, followed a few years later by the another article giving reasons why I changed my mind. While putting this section together, it occurred to me I don't often write about my own work, except perhaps for Wraeththu. I wish I had done 'work in progress' pieces throughout my career, not least because it would be interesting for me to look back and observe past practices. Perhaps I should think about that in future!

'On the Craft of Writing' includes several pieces I wrote for web sites, talks, writing classes and magazines, as well as for the Author Resources part of the Immanion Press blog. Inevitably, as most of them were created long before the tsunami rise of the internet and attendant technology, some of the advice concerning the submission of work is now a little out of date. Most publishers have web sites, and many will take electronic submissions rather than the painstakingly printed-out manuscripts that used to cost a bomb to post. Aside from that, the advice within the articles still stands, and I saw no reason to update it, since the alterations to the publishing industry need no explanation, and if a writer isn't aware of how the internet has changed the world, they must be a recluse.

I've written quite a few introductions for other writers' work, and included here are the ones I still have on my computer. Reading them again, in order to check for errors, made me want to dig out the books again – especially Pat Cadigan's *Dirty Work*. I remembered how much I loved reading those stories. The final piece in this section is the introduction I wrote for Tanith Lee's *Legenda Maris*, which Immanion Press published shortly after her death in 2015.

'Myth, Magic and Healing' includes a small selection of the articles I've written on these topics. I used to run a magical group, affiliated to the Fellowship of Isis, called Lady of the Flame Iseum, which sadly, although technically still in existence, is not very active these days. In its heyday we had a web site, which was always hungry for words. But unless someone is specifically interested in magic, many of these articles would be too specialised for the average reader. I chose the most accessible.

I hope you find much to interest you in this selection of articles. As I expect that those of you who buy this book are already fans of my work, I'd like to thank you for your continued support. Writers can't have a career without readers.

Reviews

A New Kind of Light
On Female Characters in Tanith Lee's Fiction
Review August 1996

Anyone familiar with my work and inspirations will know that Tanith Lee meant a great deal to me, as both a friend and a mentor. I wrote this review some years before I knew her as a friend, but once we had become acquainted, she was interested in my observations of her previous work, not least because she'd once been informed she had a mild form of Asperger's Syndrome. Once you've read the following, you'll see why this is relevant. You can imagine the trepidation with which I passed this review to Tanith, since I'm somewhat brutally honest in it, concerning my reactions to the characters in some of her novels. Fortunately, my views didn't offend her. Her response was that she felt she 'channelled' her characters, so in some respects had little control over what they did and said. She didn't disagree with my thoughts on the protagonists concerned.

At last! I had a premonition this was going to happen when I read the most recent Tanith Lee novel, *Reigning Cats and Dogs*. Now, it's been confirmed. Ms Lee's heroines are evolving. Perhaps I had better explain...

I have been a fan of Tanith Lee since her first novel, *The Birthgrave*, which was published by Futura in 1977. I am proud to name her as one of my inspirations. Quite a few of my friends are also into Lee's work, and more than a few of them are writers. Lately, we've all been saying that there's something about Ms Lee's more recent work that makes us feel uncomfortable. Deeper discussion revealed the source of our discomfort. Several of these books had a heart of ice, with what almost felt like a hint of misogyny. Not only that, Ms Lee's heroines seemed virtually autistic – cold and remote. They were often eternal victims, moving indifferently through the pages of the novels, simply *allowing* the most dreadful things to happen to them. Some disliked the process, others didn't seem to care. Nobody seemed to emerge from the nether end of the story having learned anything. Nobody changed.

Thinking about this in more detail, we realised it was a phenomenon often present in Tanith Lee's work to a greater or lesser degree - right from the beginning. But to illustrate my point, I will first cite two examples from her later canon: the Blood Opera sequence (*Dark Dance*, 1992; *Personal Darkness*, 1993 and *Darkness, I,* 1994, Little Brown) and *Vivia*, (1995, Little Brown).

The *Blood Opera* books are superb in style. The narrative is trimmed of all fat and there's not one word out of place. The heroine, one Rachaela Day, knows her father, whom she has never met, is a member of a mysterious family, the Scarabae. Shady lawyers pursue Rachaela to tell her this previously unknown bunch of relatives want to meet her. Rachaela has absolutely *no* curiosity about this at all, not even when it means she might discover more about her mysterious, absent father, or acquire vast amounts of wealth. There is some mention that she is afraid of the Scarabae - an instinctive fear, since her mother could give her no details about them - but Rachaela's fear is as listless as any other emotion that might occasionally haunt her otherwise unoccupied psyche. Early in the narrative, it is mentioned she was once raped at a party, but this event inspired little more than a yawn in Rachaela. She is barely human.

Eventually, Rachaela gives in lethargically to the Scarabae's request and travels to the family manse, on a remote heath near the coast. The Scarabae house is evoked in lush detail - you are drowned in the fading colours, can smell its must and incense, taste its air, hear its hidden creakings. Other members of the family too are drawn in fine detail - eccentric and puzzling oldsters, some of whom as the trilogy progresses appear to get younger. The Scarabae may be vampires, or not. They may be immortal, or not. What is certain is that they are not ordinary.

That is the premise of *Dark Dance*. A book of mysteries, secrets and scandals. I loved it. But Rachaela, I wanted to hit. Later, she is joined in the story by her stultifying daughter, Ruth; a product of an incestuous union with her father, Adamus. Ruth, like her mother, is another emotional void, only rather more dangerous. She kills the characters with whom you feel most empathy. A loathsome child.

In the second book, Rachaela falls in love (we presume that's what it is) with the mysterious, androgynous Althene, but there is little proof of feeling.

The trilogy charts the intrigues of the Scarabae family; fascinating reading with some excellent characters, but the wall-flowers at the party, the ones whose silence at the edge of the room spoils the atmosphere, are Rachaela and her daughters Ruth and Anna. The daughters are slightly more interesting than Rachaela as they appear to be psychotic, but they're hardly great conversationalists or emotional fireballs.

In *Vivia*, (Little Brown, 1995), we meet a heroine based physically on Mengin's painting of Sappho, a Pre-Raphaelite classic. (If you ever go to Manchester, visit the city gallery to drool over this painting. It's one of the most awesomely huge and atmospheric pictures I've ever seen). In the picture, which adorns the cover of the book, we see a moody and seductive Sappho staring out at us, against a backdrop of dark rocks and a heaving black sea. Bare-breasted, the figure is otherwise draped in diaphanous black cloth. She is beautiful and powerful; certainly no arid maid. A print of this painting has adorned my work-room wall as inspiration for some time. It portrays a woman who takes no shit, and I often need to be reminded of that trait. Vivia, however, is another story.

The writing again is superb, a delight to read, but the heroine is another cold enigma. Orphaned, (a blessing, her parents were vile), by plague and war, she exists alone in a frozen castle, with death all around her. After all hell was let loose in the castle, at the beginning of the book, Vivia found sanctuary in the labyrinthine cellars and caves beneath it. Here, she is *changed* by a vampiric, god-like male. Eventually, she struggles back to her bed-chamber above ground, and here falls into a death-like swoon, only to be awoken some time later by a prince. The comparison with Sleeping Beauty ends here.

Vivia is taken from her tomb-castle and embarks upon a series of adventures that happen around her. She has become vampiric, but we are never absolutely sure she is a *vampire* in the traditional sense. All well and good; the enigma is fascinating. Apathetically, Vivia feeds on young girls provided by her husband, and submits laconically to his bullying. The world of the story is captivating, and the twists of the narrative snare the attention, but if Vivia participates in any of its events it's definitely not to have fun or to experience anything. At certain points in the story, I wanted to shake the woman. 'Do something! Don't just sit there! Answer back. Stand up for yourself!'

I didn't come away from any of these books *dissatisfied*, which might sound odd, given what I've said above, but this is because Ms Lee is a superlative story-teller and a mistress of language. Still, I wondered about the woman behind the books, the writer herself. What could she be like to create this parade of stunningly frigid females?

Stylistically, they do work in a strange kind of way, especially in the novella *Nightshades* in the collection of the same name (Headline, 1993). Here we have another heroine who is 'done to' rather than 'does'. But there is some indication that Sovaz' fire has been quenched by ill-luck and an unfortunate marriage. We feel sympathy for her:

When he brought her back to the house from the tenement attic, her laughter had been stopped. Indeed, he did not see her laugh much after, except sometimes, now and again, across a room full of guests and smoke. He had her hair dyed to its original shade, her face wiped clean in readiness for expensive cosmetics. She was now extremely docile.

Reigning Cats and Dogs (Headline 1995) showed the beginning of new style of heroine for Tanith Lee. This was a slim book, and from the very first line, I was hooked. The lines quoted below are from the first paragraph and illustrate perfectly Ms Lee's dexterity with language:

'A quarter to midnight and the City lies still.

The moon stands high above the river, among the tangled spars of ships in the docks. The moon is the silver cog of the wheel of night. And the river is stained with silver like a blade.

The buildings hold up their shapes into darkness, and here and there a dull red window smoulders, but mostly the panoply of spires and hovels, domes and tenements lean black on black.'

I defy anyone not to call that poetry. The prose is rhythmic and lilting, the metre perfect. You can almost dance to it.

Reigning Cats and Dogs is a parody or imitation of a Dickensian tale, and although the story seems to take place in Victorian London, you also get the feeling you're in a completely fantastical world. The heroine, Grace, is cat-like (perhaps no coincidence she shares the name of Orlando the Marmalade Cat's wife, from the *Orlando* children's books by Katherine Hale). Also, she is *warm*. A bewitching, sorceress-whore. The tale is magical and moving – populated by colourful strumpets, beggars, thieves and moneyed gentlemen. And cats and dogs. Bast and Anubis; the cat- and jackal-headed deities of Ancient Egypt. Victorian London was never like this; a pity.

There might not seem to be a connection between ancient Egypt and historic London, but there is, and I've no doubt Tanith Lee is aware of that. (Part of the Thames is named after Isis, and there are legends that the remains of the twelfth dynasty female king, Sobhek Nofru-Re, were brought to this land in the distant past.) Grace's movement through the narrative of this novel is as graceful as the waving of a cat's tail. She is serene rather than frigid; enigmatic rather than obtuse. I *cared* about her. Were Tanith Lee's female protagonists changing?

When the Lights Go Out (Headline 1996) has confirmed it. This is a wonderful story abrim with magical realism. In some ways, it resembles the Scarabae books, in that the heroine, Hesta Web, has mysterious family connections of which she's unaware. It's what makes her different; a priestess and a sea-witch. Hesta is far more like Mengin's Sappho than poor old Vivia could ever be.

All the characters in the new novel are either funny, quirky, bizarre or bewitching. Hesta lives in a hideously fashionable house with her dreadful wine-bar-frequenting mother, Stephanie; a self-starved woman who can't bear the thought of getting old. As she *is* getting old, Hesta takes the brunt of her frustrations. The father works away on an oil rig; a ghostly presence who can't or won't amend the injustices of Hesta's life. Hesta, however, has wonderful friends, whom she loves: the fabulous Lulu – a galleon of a woman, a primal goddess, who builds up such a rapport with an obscene caller that he phones when his mother dies, so that Lulu can provide him with another, more meaningful, kind of release. Then there is Lulu's daughter, Janey, a punk-haired imp, the kind of girl I would have loved to have had as a best friend or a sister. Lulu and Janey are Hesta's sanctuary.

One night, returning home from Lulu's flat, Hesta finds the house empty, but soon discovers that Stephanie has been screwing her vile, trendy lover, Martin, in Hesta's bed, and has also been wearing her daughter's underwear for the occasion. Martin fancies Hesta rather more than he fancies Stephanie, and Hesta guesses immediately what on his mind while indulging in erotic play in her bed-room. Rightfully disgusted, Hesta has had enough and decides to run away. The following day, she goes on a day trip to the sea with Janey. Once she has visited the weird seaside resort (un-named), which is in itself a character in the book, Hesta is prepared to cut herself free from the only people who have given her life meaning. She sends a distraught Janey home without her. At first, I wondered why. Have we another emotional vacuum girl here? Ah, no. Hesta's arrival in the resort, on the last day of the Season, is pre-ordained and some instinct within her knows that.

Left alone, she wanders the old part of the town, and here witnesses a woman deliberately throw a crying baby down onto the street, where it dies in a pool of blood. She is pulled away from the scene by proto-Goth, Skilt, who appears from the shadows and explains that what Hesta has witnessed may or may not be a supernatural phenomenon. Whatever it was, the old part of the town seethes with it. Ghostly cars driven by the dead; warped graffiti (Wet Paint for example is defaced to read We Pain); naked individuals cavorting shamelessly on the beach; an old bag lady called The Duchess who pushes a gull around in a pram. No-one but the inner cabal of the resort go into the old part of town Out of Season. Interlopers who mock its traditions might find they never leave - alive.

Hesta is absorbed into Skilt's menagerie of what appears to be losers and drop-outs – all of whom have strange gifts or even paranormal powers. They live in the crumbling splendour of the Victoria Hotel, and chat about benefit cheques and life on the streets. Not for long though. It soon becomes clear that Hesta's arrival is something they've all been waiting for, and before long she outgrows the ragamuffin tribe and is drawn to the house of the mysterious boy-man, Hassinger, who seems to own the town.

Presiding over all of it is the dark, powerful presence of the winter ocean. The novel is interspersed with the phrase 'The sea breathed'. And you can hear it, sighing away in the background at every moment. This story is filled with the ancient folk-lore of the sea and those whose lives depend on it, and mythical figures stride or glide across the pages like half-seen ghosts at the corner of your eye.

To say more about the plot would spoil the book for would-be readers – and I recommend the novel to anyone. Suffice to say, the final paragraph brought tears to my eyes. Here was human warmth, community spirit and, at last a heroine who *grew*, learned and changed throughout the book. At the beginning, Hesta is a confused young girl; by the end she is Mengin's Sappho.

I can only wait impatiently for Tanith Lee's next novels. Whether she reverts to writing of cold, withered-heart women or continues to fill her books with warmth, I know I will enjoy them. But I hope to have my emotions touched, as well as my aesthetic sense.

Here is a link to a fansite that gives a thorough bibliography of Tanith's work. http://www.daughterofthenight.com/

Jack Vance:
Critical Appreciations and a Bibliography
Edited by A E Cunningham
The British Library, 2000

This is primarily a book for Vance enthusiasts, but if he is one of your favourite writers, then it is a treasure house. It is a warm and affectionate tribute, and with enough tantalising quotes from Vance's best work to attract new readers, should they take the time to read these lively and colourful essays.

Jack Vance has never quite received the public credit and attention he deserves for his contributions to sf and fantasy. He is often cited as a major influence and inspiration by many successful authors, yet most of his books have been long out of print. Often, he has been criticised for his baroque and archaic style, but to the Vance aficionado, he is a master of language, wit and imagination. Now, as Vance is in his eighties, there is renewed interest, with reprints and new editions of his work and also this collection of eleven essays. I'm glad he's still around to enjoy the well-deserved praise. Masters of the craft, many of whom are friends of Vance, contribute to this book which, as Terry Dowling puts it in his offering 'Fruit From the Tree of Life', ' ...isn't intended as a book of critical essays, but rather as a selection of heartfelt and informed appreciations.' And so they are.

Contributors such as Harlan Ellison, Gene Wolfe, Dan Simmons and David Langford indulge themselves in telling us why they love Vance's writing. David Mathew's 'From Phade to Wayness: the Changing Role of Women' discusses Vance's approach to female characters throughout his work, A. E. Cunningham gives us a full bibliography (to help track down those out-of-print titles you've always wanted to read) and Charles F Miller's contribution 'Publishing Jack Vance' documents the writer's career. There is also an article by Vance himself, which gives fascinating glimpses into his life – a very rich, full and varied one, to be sure. Is there anything this man hasn't done? The photo archive spans the last century, from pictures of Vance on his mother's knee in 1916 to a book signing in 1990.

As a fan of Vance myself, I devoured this book gleefully, relishing the insights into his life and work. It makes me look to my shelf of Vance books and decide which one I'll take down first to re-read. How can anyone resist a writer who could pen the lines: *'While we are alive we should sit among colored lights and taste good wines, and discuss our adventures in far places; when we are dead, the opportunity is past'*?

Jack Vance died on May 26th, 2013 at the age of 96. Since then, (and a while before his death too), his books have been steadily brought back into print by small press enthusiasts, as well as larger publishers. Here is a link to a bibliography online:
http://www.fantasticfiction.co.uk/v/jack-vance/

Kushiel's Dart:
Kushiel's Legacy Book One
Jacqueline Carey
TOR, 2001

Kushiel's Dart *takes fantasy into shadowy exotic corners it rarely dares to tread. The standard of the writing is so high, it's hard to believe this is a first novel. There are some genuinely shocking moments, but even the darkest of them are written with skilful elegance. The characters are captivating and the plot cleverly convoluted. I read many new writers, but few of them capture my attention as Jacqueline Carey has. A writer to watch – as the cliché goes – but more importantly a writer to read.*

Quote sent to TOR Books for *Kushiel's Dart*, January 2000

Every so often, a publisher will send me a novel in the hope I'll read it and provide a comment for the cover. Most of these are from new fantasy writers. I have to say that the bulk of them are run of the mill, formulaic fantasy that have nothing new or exciting to add to the genre. I won't endorse something I don't like, so I adopt the 'no comment' stance. But occasionally, just occasionally, I'll be sent something a bit more interesting. *Kushiel's Dart* falls into this category.

When the bound proofs for this novel arrived a couple of weeks ago, I thought, 'This is so big, I'll never have time to read it, even if it's brilliant'. But, as it happened, I had a new year's cold and went to bed early one night feeling a bit rough. Not wanting to sleep immediately, I picked up *Kushiel's Dart* and started to read. From page one, I was hooked and since then have made time to finish it, all 600 pages.

The background to the story gives a new take on the fallen angel myth. It's set mainly in a country called Terre D'Ange, (Land of the Angel), which appears to be an alternate France.

All the noble families in this land claim descent from a company of fallen angels, who were loyal to the 'Blessed Elua'. Elua was an angel 'born' from the blood of Yeshua ben Yosef (Jesus) and the tears of the Magadalene. Several angels went against the will of the One God to be companions to Elua and from their interaction with humanity the noble families of Terre D'Ange derived. At one stage Elua was taken into captivity by the king of Persis and his follower, Naamah, offered herself to the king to secure the angel's freedom. Naamah was quite happy to offer her body for coin whenever Elua was a bit short, and from this legend a cult of sacred prostitution grew. In the City of Elua stands the Night Court, thirteen houses of pleasure, each with their own particular 'flavour', in which the servants of Naamah ply their trade.

The protagonist of the novel is Phedre, sold to House Cereus of the Night Court as a child. The first part of the story describes Phedre's childhood in Cereus and her eventual transference to the house of mysterious noble-man, Anafiel Delauney. All of Naamah's servants have a 'marque', a tattoo that runs up the spine. When they start their careers, the marque is small. Its completion means freedom. Each addition to the marque is paid for by patron gifts, private donations from satisfied clients that do not go into the House coffers. Delauney buys Phedre's marque. It means she will be part of his household, subject to pleasing the clients Delauney finds for her, until her marque is completed. Then she will be a free woman.

But there is more to Phedre than merely being a servant of Naamah. She is marked by 'Kushiel's Dart', a mote of scarlet in the iris of her left eye. This is the sign of an anguissette, a woman who enjoys pain, who more than enjoys pain. She has the mark of the angel Kushiel upon her. Delauney recognises what this mark means and how it proposes to make Phedre's talents much in demand among the somewhat dissipated nobility of Terre D'Ange.

The blurb I received with the book told me I was in for a

darkly erotic read, but for nearly a hundred pages matters sexual are mentioned only by implication. Even Phedre's training at House Valerian, which specialises in S&M, is not described in detail. Still, I could tell the book was building up to something, and I wasn't wrong. Chapter Two, for example, begins with the sentence, 'I remember the moment when I discovered pain'.

Some readers might find the descriptions of Phedre's encounters with her clients difficult reading. Even I winced at times as I read about Phedre's craving for humiliation and torture from both men and women. The sex scenes are eventually described in detail, but even though you might want to flinch away from the book sometimes, the writing remains elegant and understated. What is implied shocks more than what is said. You can only admire a writer who rejects out and out visceral, horror tactics and carefully words these scenes for maximum effect. It requires far more skill than crass description of terrible acts. Still, some readers might find Phedre's perversions unsettling. Despite Delauney's nobility and beauty, he is still a pimp and Phedre a whore. They might gloss it up with posh terms and allusions to sacred calling, but at the end of the day it's paid sex, bodies as commodities. Delauney uses Phedre, and also his other 'pupil', Alcuin, a beautiful boy, to glean snippets of political information from unwary clients in bed – or the torture chamber. This he utilises in his machinations at court.

I must admit that at first I found Delauney's actions despicable and Phedre's pathetic and sad, but the story is so compelling, you're carried along with it, and once the novel really gets going, the weird sex seems almost incidental. Phedre eventually learns that she and Delauney have been playing a very dangerous game, which leads inevitably to death and terror. She is obsessed by the beautiful Melisande Shahrizai, who is consummately wicked, with a lust for power and propensity for intrigue. Melisande does quite a few wicked, if not evil, things to Phedre, (the scene with the flechettes takes a strong stomach), but is perhaps more deadly out of the bedroom than in it.

Not wanting to spoil the story for those who haven't read it, I'll only say that Phedre ends up being sold as a slave, sent to a far land, and there learns even more about treason brewing at home. The rest of the book describes how she and her companion, Joscelin, eventually escape, find their way home through many dangers, and become involved in the politics of war to save Terre D'Ange from invaders and traitors. Phedre's unique talents play a considerable part along the way.

The plot is incredibly convoluted with betrayals and double betrayals leading the reader through a maze of character motives and desires. This brief résumé can only skim across the surface of the many historical stories and sub-plots that bring the book to life. The background and history are so well thought out, you'd be forgiven for believing it's a piece of European history that somehow you've never read or heard about. *Kushiel's Dart*, in fact, reads more like an alternative history than fantasy, because in fantasy we are used to having a magical element to the story. Apart from a couple of psychic characters, who are not overplayed, and the timely appearance of an omenic beast, the otherworldly is absent until near the end of the story. When it does arrive, it seems a little out of place. That is probably my only gripe with the book.

All the way through, the plot takes place very much in the physical realm, and it isn't until Phedre has to cross the sea to Alba (presumably England) to drum up support for her country that a supernatural element intervenes. This is in the form of the Master of the Straits, a kind of sea god/elemental who prevents boats crossing between the two countries. I was taken by surprise when the Master of the Straits made his first appearance as a huge watery face rising up out of the ocean, creating storms and chaos. Later, the Master is given some kind of rationale, when Phedre discovers exactly who and what he is, but even so this part didn't sit well with me, as it seemed a bit unlikely. The book stands up splendidly without this more fantastical aspect, so why insert it at such a late stage? It's still well-written and interesting, but seemed to belong to a different book.

Reviews traditionally give comparisons to other books, to provide readers with a yard stick as to style and content, so these are my opinions. There are parallels within *Kushiel's Dart* to some of my own work, especially novels like *Burying the Shadow* and *Sign for the Sacred*. I was also reminded of the early work of Elizabeth Hand, specifically *Winterlong* (Spectra, 1990), and also a little known but wonderful alternative history novel called *A Mirror For Princes* by Tom de Haan (Arena Arrow, 1988). As for movies, there are elements of *Dangerous Liasons* (or *Cruel Intentions*, if you want to go for the Hollywood update) and also *La Reine Margot*.

Jacqueline Carey clearly has a fondness for her beautiful, fey, bisexual characters and their unusual sexuality. She has captured the amorality of the fallen angels perfectly through their hybrid descendants, who are capable of the ultimate compassion and the ultimate cruelty. At the end of the book, the author does leave room for a further novel, but this is no series cliff-hanger. The dénouement is satisfying and complete.

Naming no names, I have seen other writers begin their careers with exotic and/or quirky novels, who eventually seem to cave in to pressure from the publishing industry to tread more conventional turf. I hope this doesn't happen with Jacqueline Carey. The space she's writing in is limitless and there are far too many dull, traditional novels out there. Fantasy needs writing like this, authors who aren't afraid to look into the dark and strip away the fluff and gloss of tweeness. Fantasy doesn't have to be staid and safe. I'd rather go for adult, exciting and strange any day.

In the original novel, there was no indication that this was part of a

series. Subsequently, Carey wrote many novels set in the world of Kushiel's Dart. There are too many to list here, but here is a link to a bibliography online
http://www.fantasticfiction.co.uk/c/jacqueline-carey/

The Daughters of Bast:
The Hidden Land
By Sarah Isidore
Avon, USA, 1999

(Review 2000)

It's obvious that a book with a title like this one is going to attract my attention, as I've recently, with Louise Coquio, published a non-fiction book on the Egyptian goddesses Bast and Sekhmet. A couple of friends of mine had mentioned the Isidore book to me and eventually I got around to buying it. For a long time I've been meaning to write a novel, or series of novels, based on Egyptian material, especially Bast and Sekhmet, so I awaited the arrival of *Daughters of Bast: The Hidden Land* with trepidation. Had someone got there before me, and used enough of the Bast material to render a book of my own impossible?

Happily, I don't think so. The Bast of this novel is purely a fantasy goddess and bears little resemblance to the historical deity.

It took me a while to read this book as the arrival of *Kushiel's Dart* by first novelist Jacqueline Carey interrupted the proceedings – it was a book I had to read straight away. Two reasons for that; firstly, I'd been asked to provide a comment for the cover of the book and, secondly, from page one the author's voice hooked into me and wouldn't let go. By contrast, Sarah Isidore's writing is competent, grammatically correct and flowing, but the style and voice didn't have the impact of Carey's.

However, once *Kushiel's Dart* had come to its dramatic conclusion, I went back to the Isidore. The story opens with a young Celtic girl, Veleda, freeing a cat destined to become a sacrifice in a Druid ritual. The cat is no ordinary beast (obviously so, as the domestic feline wasn't common in Europe at that time) and rewards her by leading her into the otherworld, where she meets the cat-headed goddess, Bast, who tells her she has a great destiny. Veleda, being the foster-daughter of a powerful Druidess, is aware of Bast's existence. Her people have had contact with the Egyptian nation. And, like the reader, she wonders why an eastern deity should have an interest in her. We are told that Bast's evil 'sister' Sekhmet wants to bring blood and destruction to the whole of what will one day be Europe, through the agency of the Roman Empire. It will be Veleda's task to prevent this.

This, for me, is where the story fell down and where I have to go into lecture mode about a subject quite dear to me. Anyone with a smattering of knowledge about Egyptian deities will know that Sekhmet was not regarded as an evil force in particular. She was an Eye of the Sun, the power of Ra, who was responsible for smiting the pharaoh's enemies. Although she did have the power to inflict disease, (the hot fetid time before the annual Inundation was seen as her stalking ground), she was also a goddess of healing. Most of her priests were also physicians. Sekhmet was a power that could be petitioned for help in times of great need, but historically she had no 'evil' agenda of her own. Admittedly, one of her legends states that she once went on a human slaughtering spree, but this was because Ra had sent her out to chastise them for their lack of respect. Therefore, there seems to me to be no justification for casting her as some kind of bad fairy, who wants to inflict pain and destruction for its own sake. Also, I can't believe, even in fiction, that an Egyptian deity would manifest in the world through either the Romans or the Celts. It just doesn't make sense. Why not just send the Egyptian nation out to kill everybody? At least they worship Sekhmet, so presumably are more on her frequency.

Apart from the initial introduction to Bast and the continued presence of the talking cat, the rest of the story concerns

Veleda's training as a Druid, the battles of Julius Caesar against various Celtic tribes and the inter-tribe squabbling that undermines the Celts' position. If the author wanted to use a feline deity to underpin the plot, there is a Celtic goddess who could have assumed the role, and it wouldn't have jarred far so much. The presence and intervention of Bast in it seems needless. Veleda, as a powerful Druid seeress in her own right, could have performed her role in the plot just as effectively without it. The novel is not a bad book, and as I said before the early European history is well-researched, but I'm disappointed that it's a story about the Roman conquest masquerading as a story about Bast. As this is the first of a series, perhaps more of the Egyptian material will come in later, but it doesn't seem to me as if the author has much of a grasp of the character of the Egyptian gods.

Bast is cast as a gentle benign moon goddess, which is really a modern misinterpretation. In the novel, she is in conflict with her warlike 'sister' Sekhmet, who wants only to feast on human blood and pain, and doesn't care how she gets it. Perhaps, if the author had referred to the legend of Ra becoming annoyed with hmanity's treatment of him, and had used this as the justification for Sekhmet's aggression, it might have worked better for me. However, why Ra would be annoyed with Celts, who didn't worship him in the first place, would still need quite a lot more justification. Possible, perhaps, in fiction, but it would require careful planning. Also, Bast was never a 'sister' of Sekhmet. Some modern pagans see Bast and Sekhmet as two aspects of one goddess, which is not the case. All Egyptian gods can, in one way, be seen as a single entity with multiple faces, as they were regarded as *neteru*, which simplistically can be translated as names of god. Bast is therefore a *neter* of the great creative principle of the universe, as is Sekhmet, but they do have individual characteristics. The Egyptian belief system wasn't dualistic, with good and evil deities. Even Set, the feared god of chaos, who certainly had some less than benign legends attached to him, was not regarded as the opposite of creator or fertility gods, such as Amun or Osiris. They were all part of the same thing, different faces of nature, creation and the universe.

The motherly moon goddess Bast in 'The Hidden Land', and the demonic, power-mad Sekhmet, are invented deities that share only the name of the originals. Here are a few reasons why. Bast was originally a ferocious lioness goddess, almost identical in nature to Sekhmet. It wasn't until later in Egyptian history that she transformed into a domestic cat-headed form and acquired a less fearsome aspect. Like Sekhmet, she is an Eye of Ra, even in her current form. Cats can be picked up and stroked, but they can also lash out, hissing and spitting, and Bast shares these qualities. Like a cat, she can be indifferent and aloof, and even those who work with her magically or religiously would say that she has two sides to her character. As for her being a moon goddess, this is a Greek idea. The Greeks mistakenly equated Bast with their moon goddess, Artemis, an aspect that stuck with the cat goddess, and was elaborated upon by nineteenth century western occultists. But if Bast has a gentle side, historically it is the warming rays of the sun, which nurtures growth, as opposed to the searing desert heat of Sekhmet. It has to be said that if a goddess has had a certain aspect imposed upon her, which has remained in place for two thousand years, then it must inevitably have become part of her. Therefore, I wouldn't take anyone to task now if they saw Bast in this way, but in an historical novel, set in the times of the Roman conquest, long before Victorian magicians got their hands on ancient material, it just doesn't stand up.

Sekhmet was a fierce and terrifying goddess, but not in the way Sarah Isidore portrays her. To understand why some of the Egyptians' gods were so ferocious, we need to understand the way they lived and viewed the world. For this, we have only to look at the land of Eygpt itself, the Two Lands. The thin belt of fertile ground (the Black Land) that hugs the Nile seems almost fragile in comparison with the vast, inhospitable deserts (the

Red Land) that surround it. Imagine living in those surroundings, every day seeing the sun, itself regarded as a god, rise and sink into the punishing, almost lifeless wastes beyond the Black Land. Surely the Red Land was the domain of the gods, and what kinds of gods held sway there? Lions lived in the desert, where people could not, so it must have made sense to them to give some of their gods a leonine aspect. There are a lot of lion-headed deities in Egyptian belief. And any deity deriving from the desert must be as dangerous. This is the foundation from where Sekhmet arose. Lions lived in the gods' domain and because they were tolerated, and even thrived there, they were therefore perhaps servants of the gods, if not godlike themselves. Sekhmet was a personification of the sun's heat, capable of killing as much as of nurturing life, a manifestation of conditions in the natural world. But she was not regarded as evil. Her character was like a lion's, a necessary and intrinsic part of nature. It was respected and perhaps feared, but venerated too, and when people were sick, they turned to Sekhmet and her physician priests for help.

Near the end of *The Daughters of Bast*, Bast joins forces with the Celtic goddess, Anu. When Veleda visits the otherworld, she finds the two goddesses together, united in the desire to stop Sekhmet's evil plan. Again, this didn't feel right to me. It's hard to explain without going into detail about occult traditions, but goddesses are not humans, who can drop in on each other and enlist a bit of support when it's needed. They are frequencies of energy, given faces by humans who choose to interact with them. In many fantasy novels, gods are portrayed as petty, very human creatures, who interfere in human concerns, but it's the other way around. From my own experiences as a practitioner of magic, I've come to believe that humans use god energy in their own machinations, but the gods don't act independently. Now, if Julius Caesar had decided to petition the Egyptian goddess Sekhmet to expedite his campaigns in Europe, *that* would have made more sense.

OK, this is a novel, and in fiction authors are allowed to make things up and stretch reality. But to create good fantasy – literary fantasy, as in the Carey book I mentioned earlier - research has to be grounded in authenticity, just so it's believable, and frankly, the Egyptian material in *The Daughters of Bast* isn't. This is a shame, because the historical detail concerning the battles and politics of early Europe are clearly authentic.

The end of the book, which I obviously won't fully reveal so as not to spoil it for potential readers, leads to a new generation touched by Bast. It would have been a good time to move the story to Egypt, and the characters involved in the denouement would have made this credible and logical, but for some reason Isidore takes them to Ireland instead. There is evidence that the Romans brought certain Egyptian beliefs to England, mainly the worship of Isis, but there is no historical mention of Bast in this respect.

Although there have been a few mainstream novels about ancient Egypt, it hasn't been touched upon much in fantasy. There is room for a mighty, sprawling epic, rich in exotic imagery and dark magic, but *The Daughters of Bast* isn't it.

The Hidden Library of Tanith Lee:
Themes and Subtexts from Dionysos to the Immortal Gene
by Mavis Haut
Macfarland & Co, 2001

In comparison with the lively Jack Vance tribute I reviewed recently, this is a far drier book, with a serious academic slant. For die-hard Tanith Lee fans, it's a book that you'd most likely want to dip into occasionally, but it is not an easy or chatty read.

Haut examines Lee's early and middle period works exhaustively, discussing recurring motifs and symbols in great detail. It's interesting to share Haut's analysis of Ms Lee's use of folklore, fairy tales, Tarot and pagan lore – among other things. Each chapter concentrates on certain novels that share themes or worlds, and covers all but one of Lee's books up to the *Blood Opera* sequence. (Why was *Days of Grass* omitted, I wonder?)

I was surprised to find no mention in this book concerning Tanith Lee's sometimes curiously bloodless and emotionally autistic heroines, her apparent distance from (some of) her characters. After all, it's these qualities that add to the mystique of her writing. But then, her earlier characters were not quite as dour and damaged as some that have appeared in more recent works. Haut refers often to Ms Lee's characters being Dionysian, and perhaps some of the earlier ones are, but in their sometimes lofty ascetism, their abstractedness, they seem more like Apollonians. This invokes the literary and philosophical concept of the rational versus the irrational, order versus the chaotic, ascetic versus the hedonistic. However, there are many interpretations of this dichotomy, and if we look at Lee's heroines as being Chthonic and dark – another interpretation of Dionysian, I suppose they fit the bill.

In my view, however, Dionysians celebrate life in a free, almost childlike manner, and this description does not really fit the majority of Lee's characters, especially the women, who are sometimes so removed from meaningful contact with others, they can only be described as 'anti-life'.

In the conclusion, Haut explains how the constrictions of space within the book precluded her discussing Tanith Lee's later work, which is perhaps why there is no assessment of the development of her treatment of characters. I would like to see a book that studies the difficulty of some of these characters, which I've heard is one of the reasons some readers are put off Lee's work. Haut stresses the need for more examination of this prolific and vivid writer and I couldn't agree more. Tanith Lee is a phenomenon and, whether you like her style or not, and whether her writing makes you feel uncomfortable or not, she's one of most important living fantasists.

At the end of the book, you'll find an interview between Haut and Lee, which I found the most fascinating section. Within it, Lee gives details of an unwritten fourth novel in her *Blood Opera* sequence, which the vagaries of the publishing industry have so far prevented being commissioned.

For the Tanith Lee enthusiast, this is a very interesting book, and in some ways poses more questions than it answers. It discusses her work from a lofty, academic position, but – to me – didn't quite get to the heart of this intriguing writer. Also, at the price of £30 or so, the book is somewhat expensive for what you get.

Alexander:
Flawed Masterpiece
Oliver Stone, 2004

Like everyone else who discovered at a young age Mary Renault's extraordinary novel, *The Persian Boy*, I awaited the release of Oliver Stone's epic *Alexander* with huge impatience. I'd read in film magazines and online that Stone intended to convey honestly Alexander the Great's bisexuality, and that the character of Bagoas, a Persian eunuch of extreme beauty, who was given to Alexander following his conquest of Babylon, would be present in the movie.

The Persian Boy was one of my greatest influences as a young writer, right up there with the work of Tanith Lee, Jane Gaskell, Jack Vance and Michael Moorcock. While it is not a fantasy, (although a lot of people would argue that it is, since Renault fleshed out immensely the scant historical facts), the first person narrative, the lush descriptions of an exotic lost world and the subtle sensuality of Bagoas's relationship with Alexander captivated me utterly. I read Jane Gaskell's *Atlan* series round about the same time, and perceived similarities in the stories – not least in the authors' styles – even though one story was set in the ancient world of our own reality and the other was set in the imagined realm of Atlantis. So, the idea of one of my favourite books being brought to life in a film, if only partly, was exciting to say the least.

There is no doubt in my mind that Stone used *The Persian Boy* as a resource, because I wasn't alone in spotting some direct references to the novel. And yes, Bagoas was in the movie, albeit without having one line of dialogue (in the theatrical cut). But did it live up to my vision?

The answer is both yes and no, but I loved it regardless. Therefore, I've been astounded by the savage response from what appears to be the majority of movie-goers against the film. I mean, it does have its flaws, (and in all honesty sometimes quite big ones), but I really can't understand the 'most awful film ever made' tag that it's acquired – even from people whose movie tastes are very similar to mine. One friend, who I imagined would quite enjoy it, found it almost impossible to watch and was extremely bored by it. Yet other friends really loved it. So what was in there to elicit such extremes of reaction?

The narrative structure of the film certainly isn't conventional, nor particularly tight. In fact, 'loose' might be a better description. There is also a lot of talking, which some viewers found tedious. A large part of the film is narrated by Anthony Hopkins' character of Ptolemy:

> *"Now in his dotage, Ptolemy is shown periodically puttering about his palace, dictating his memoirs of Alexander and thereby filling in the details of his life and campaigns that Stone and his co-writers choose not to include in the flashbacks that form the bulk of the film."*
>
> From a review by Eric D Snider
http://www.ericdsnider.com/movies/alexander/

For some reason, Stone put an immense flashback to Alexander's earlier life in the last third of the film, which I personally thought would have worked better put in the right place chronologically, since it detracts from the forward motion of the story: obviously.

A lot of reviewers thought the film was confusing, as it focused on some events in the great leader's life while leaving out others, which were important to the understanding of Alexander as a human being. His rise to power is not shown at all. You go from seeing him as a relative nobody in his father, King Phillip of Macedonia's court, to commanding a great army at the famous battle of Gaugamela. I can understand why people wondered what the script writers were doing when constructing the story of Alexander's life for film.

Alexander's sexuality is referred to uncompromisingly, as is that of his fellow countrymen, which some viewers clearly found 'difficult', but it's not shown overtly. At the other extreme, some reviewers were even annoyed about that too, especially the fact that the only erotic scene in the movie is between Alexander and the Bactrian wife he takes:

> *"Her name is Roxane (Rosario Dawson), a Babylonian girl, (sic) and though the only sex scene in the film is between her and Alexander, it is never suggested that he actually loves her. His fondness for the menfolk is given much more weight, even though wariness on the part of Warner Bros. forced Stone to keep that aspect from getting too graphic. This fact will be met with appreciation by those who don't enjoy seeing gay sex scenes, of course, but it does seem silly to make a film about a gay historical figure, keep referring to his gayness, show him pining for his gay lovers, and then never actually let him be gay."*

From the review by Eric D Snider, as above.

> *"Leto [who plays Hephaistion, Alexander's 'childhood sweetheart'] spends much of the film done up to look like a wet hippie, while Stone makes a good case for gays in the military. That the two are romantically involved is blatantly obvious, but the film seems scared to death to show them kissing or actually getting naked. Instead we're back to that narrator fellow who insists that they're each other's soul mate since obviously Stone is too inept or afraid to get down to showing it. At some point Jared Leto's faux-feminine performance simply becomes annoying, as do their furtively longing glances. Stone is a homosexual cock-tease who ought to quit spending so much time beating us over the head with his characters' homosexuality if he's never going to really put it on display.*

It's a ridiculous game that insults the historical fact behind the people whose story he's telling as well as the intelligence of his extremely bored audience."

From Joshua Taylor's review on Cinema Blend
http://www.cinemablend.com/review.php?id=759

I understand that sex scenes between Alexander and his gay lovers were filmed but never made it to the final print, for the reason cited above concerning Warner Bros. There's one kiss – between Alexander and Bagoas – and that is hardly a private, tension-charged moment since it takes place in front of a huge crowd and at their encouragement. The scene with Roxane is probably the most wince-making in the entire movie, and to me seemed 'tacked on', as if the director was nervous about Alexander's hitherto exclusively gay leanings and had forebodings about the response he'd get to it. Let's just say this part of the film didn't convince me.

Another thing that whipped viewers into a frenzy was the fact that the majority of the actors had UK and Irish regional accents. Most thought this was laughable, but I have to say it actually worked for me, and I didn't find it irritating at all. While it is obviously not historically accurate, it's far preferable than just having everyone with an American accent, which is what usually happens in movies. (Although I do think that since *Gladiator* (Ridley Scott, 2000), and the cast's British accents in that, a lot of directors appear to think that the Brit sound is somehow more appropriate for historical epics – and maybe more conducive to realistic atmosphere – than the American. Think both *King Arthur* (Antoine Fuqua 2004) and *Troy* (Wolfgang Petersen, 2004) here too. I think Colin Farrell made a good Alexander, even with the Irish accent.

Angelina Jolie, as Alexander's mother, also came under flak. This was both for her camped up pagan ways and her accent (a sort of faux-Russian, which I actually liked, even though it was camp). You could tell the actress was having a whale of a time with the part, and the character comes across as a flamboyant, self-consciously smouldering sort of creature. She wasn't unbelievable to me, but that might just be because of the circles I've mixed in! (I'm an old Goth, remember. Think Eighties.) If reviewers were going to get nit-picky about her part, they should perhaps have mentioned the fact she describes the biting risks of a snake that's actually a constrictor, but not many people seemed to notice that, having been brought to a flabbergasted halt by her accent and unable to go further with the criticism:

> "[Jolie], who vamps it up like Theda Bara reborn and sports an accent as grotesque as the one her father John Voight did in "Anaconda," is bizarre in the worst sense..."
>
> From 'One Guy's Opinion' web site
> (page now taken down)

And a slightly kinder take from the same Eric Snider review quoted above:

> "Alexander's creepy relationship with Mom is one of the film's several giggling points, and in fact Angelina Jolie's entire performance is, I think, destined to become a camp classic, up there with Faye Dunaway in "Mommie Dearest." (Jolie is one year older than Farrell, by the way.) She screams, schemes and moans with wild abandon, not to mention her fondness for snakes and her indescribable accent."

There were also complaints about the battle scenes – too much of them or too little – and the soaked colouring of the conflict set in India with the war elephants, which was reminiscent of a style used in Hero (Yimou Zhang, 2002). One friend of mine, incidentally, who watched it with me, said he kept expecting some cave trolls to come lumbering into that scene. It was somewhat reminiscent of the battle scenes in Return of the King (Peter Jackson, 2003), I suppose.

43

So, given that I don't entirely disagree with all the criticisms, why did I come away from this movie satisfied when so many others didn't? To work this out, I have to return to another recent epic; *King Arthur* (mentioned above).

Friends of mine were helplessly appalled by the liberties that were taken with the enshrined mythology of Arthur and his knights, and denounced the movie as a travesty. But when I watched it, it occurred to me to forget about the influences and just watch it for its own sake. If you're not busy being offended by the fact it's not Malory, the film stands up fairly well as a fantasy epic. I think it's partly the same with *Alexander*. Apart from the technical buffs, who seem to enjoy congratulating themselves on how cleverly they can pick the film's structure apart, a lot of people who've criticised the film are aficionados of Alexandrian history, (often "self-styled", it has to be said). These viewers cannot help but get hugely upset that their particular vision and beliefs are challenged or knocked over or just ... well... *not done how they would have done them*. If you're really into something, you'll always take issue with the way it's filmed: look at all the LOTR fanatics who detested Peter Jackson's excellently made adaptations of the books.

Alexander was always going to be an ambitious and perhaps risky project, and even at three hours' length, Stone was never going to be able to tell the whole story. Perhaps some of his judgements concerning what he included and what he didn't can be questioned, but I still think it's a good film and certainly not the 'worst ever made'. For me, *Alexander* had an enchanting otherworldly atmosphere that stayed with me beyond the end credits. I got the same feeling when I first saw *Fellowship of the Ring* (Peter Jackson, 2001). Somehow, Stone made me believe in his world, flaws and all. It will never please anyone who likes fast-paced stories, because a lot of it is slow and meandering, but ultimately whether it's good or not will always be down to personal taste. I wouldn't even say 'go and see and judge for yourself', in the confident belief that my view is the right one, because I know that even those of you who like the same things I do won't all buy into Stone's vision. Some of you will like it, some won't, and it really is all subjective.

"Stone has, in my humble opinion, crafted a great film that will be appreciated by those with an open mind and patience. I have always had a high tolerance for long movies, and I think many films would be better if they were willing to add another half-hour. Is the movie boring? Yes. But you know what, pacing is over-rated. Pacing is important to people who have trouble keeping awake at the movies. If you have the ability to remain focused on one thing for three hours, then you just might love "Alexander". "2001" is a poorly-paced, boring movie, but it's still one of the greatest films ever made. [Alexander is] a great film for those who will let it be."

From a viewer's comment on the Internet Movie
Database http://www.imdb.com

Well, I'm not quite sure the person who wrote that should have used the word 'boring' in that context exactly. I think they just mean 'slow paced'. But anyway… I quoted it just to show that not everyone hates the film. I won't quote any of the more astounding detrimental remarks, since most of them are bigoted and offensive in the extreme, at which the most politically incorrect person in the world would balk. Check out the immense forum on *Alexander* on IMDB if you're interested, but brace yourself!

Back to Bagoas for *The Persian Boy* fans. Before I end this piece, he has to be mentioned, not least because this historical character has a huge following online. After watching *Alexander*, I looked at various groups and forums that had formed devoted to this character, and found there the same kinds of rants for and against the movie as can be found elsewhere on the web. (Perhaps the most amusing was from a woman who believes herself to be a reincarnation of Alexander, and who devoutly insists he never had male lovers. Hmmm, ok, love. Whatever you want.) The actor chosen to play the part of Bagoas is perfect for it, even if he doesn't conform to everyone's vision of what this beautiful creature looked like. His presence is mostly implied rather than graphically depicted. Apart from his fabulous dance scene, and the aforementioned kiss, he mostly hovers at the edges of the film, administering to the troubled Alexander at all times. Sometimes, only his hands are in shot, and we get the briefest glimpse of his face to let us know he's in the scene. He's the one dabbing water on Alexander's face on his death bed, for example, and after Alexander murders one of his closest friends in a drunken rage, and is tearfully ranting to Hephaistion in his chambers, he's lying in Bagoas's arms, even though you only see the arms. This is subtly done, and although all Bagoas fans would obviously have liked to see more of him, I think his part was done fairly well.

I was looking forward to the DVD release, which I hoped would include a lot of the footage that never made it into the movie, including more of Bagoas, but in this month's (February 2005) *Total Film* magazine I read that although Stone plans to do a different version of the film, it's implied he's going to cut even more of the references to Alexander's homo/bisexuality. There was no mention of the other criticisms that have been levelled against the film. Stone must *really* have been scared by those nasty reviews then! The fact is, he couldn't win. For some, *Alexander* was too gay, and for others not gay enough.

My personal opinion is that the director was brave in making this film, and has – while weathering terrific storms of disapproval – opened the way for other projects that address the subject seriously and honestly. For someone who writes a fair amount of homoerotic material, and who has seriously doubted any of her work ever being filmed because of it, this is a welcome thing.

All I can say is, Mr Stone, please ignore the detractors and give the multitude of your fans out there, who are not offended or frightened by what you tried to convey, (and they are legion), the cut of *Alexander* they'd really like to see.

In fact Stone did eventually bring out a vastly extended Director's Cut on DVD that includes more of Bagoas, and Alexander's relationship with him.

Lost Worlds

Clark Ashton Smith
Panther, 1974
(Review from 2005)

One of the reasons I fell in love with Clark Ashton Smith's work as a young teenager was his colourful use of language. As a fledgling writer I was impressed by arcane and unusual words, and reading Smith's baroque stories was like being drip fed word-honey, perhaps laced with some exotic and narcotic alcohol. I came to Smith via H P Lovecraft, and those fabulous old Panther Books editions, when the whole school of weird tale-spinners all came back into print. Lovecraft hardly reined himself in on the convoluted sentences, but Smith blazed on to greater excesses. And the things he described...

The lost worlds included in this collection imply a feverish imagination to say the least. Some could best be termed fantasy, others science fiction, but all are set in vivid and uncanny landscapes, some on the edge of destruction beneath the light of dying suns, peopled by arrogant warrior kings and conniving magicians. They are also horror stories in the literal sense. Most of the tales describe dooms of various grotesque sorts, although there are a couple of tales that are reminiscent of Jack Vance in their somewhat humorous tone. In fact, I think Vance's *Dying Earth* stories probably owe more than a nod to Mr Smith.

Revisiting the stories after a long time away provided an interesting new perspective. They come across as slightly camp now, but still with the power to captivate. I might be smiling more than gasping nowadays, but the insanely opulent prose is still a treat. The lost worlds in question include Xiccarph (another planet) and forgotten realms of our own world, Zothique, Atlantis, Hyperborea and Averoigne. To round up the collection there are also some stories under the heading of 'others', which are random exotic corners of Smith's imagination.

Like Lovecraft, Smith invented a mythos, since most of his worlds are tentatively connected, and their upper (and lower) realms are populated by gods and demigods of horrific attributes. The Cthulhu Mythos became a bona fide magical system espoused by chaos magicians in the late twentieth century, and it would be interesting to see Smith's mythos undergo the same process. Lovecraft, who had no belief in the occult, would have been disgusted if he knew what would happen to his material, but I think Clark Ashton Smith would have been more sympathetic, if not pleased. There is an atmosphere within his writing that implies at a subtle level he's in awe of his creations rather than simply repulsed by them. If the god Zhothaqquah and his fellows aren't worse than Cthulhu's crew, they're on a level. Batlike, slobbering, slavering, shuffling... multiple appendages appearing loathsomely from bloated amorphous shapes... you get the picture. Aphrodite they are not.

I identified with the outsider in Smith and can remember the huge impact a particular paragraph from *Planet of the Dead* had on me when I was about fourteen. I just have to quote some of it:

> *'For Melchoir was one of those who are born with an immedicable distaste for all that is present or near at hand; one of those who have drunk too lightly of oblivion and have not wholly forgotten the transcendent glories of other aeons.... The earth is too narrow for such, and the compass of mortal time is too brief; and paucity and barrenness are everywhere; and in all places their lot is a never ending weariness.'*

Yes! I thought as I read that, heart swelling. I was the weird kid at school who was into weird things. I wanted to live in Ancient Greece or Egypt. In Smith, I found a mentor. His worlds were like those vanished aeons, and I could immerse myself in his violet prose and just be... somewhere else. The fact that most of the stories were so doom laden and grim also appealed to the angry teen in me.

There are no kindly wizards in *Lost Worlds*, but a horde of necromancers, sorcerers, torturers and dark priests of the most perverse kind. They inhabit surreal and immense mansions and palaces, waited upon by peculiar familiars and automata. In the darkness, they scheme the annihilation of their rivals. They breed strange and deadly flowers, or decant poisons. They appear dead, sitting immobile as liches on obsidian thrones, but then exact horrible revenge on those who come to loot their silent, dust-wreathed halls. The gods of these stories are similarly without benign aspects. They are like the demons of Tibetan lore, kept at bay by clever magicians, but eager to inflict monstrous torment upon their worshippers whenever the opportunity presents itself. The kings are mostly tyrants, and there are few female characters, other than the occasional limpid maiden who's the beloved of a story's protagonist, and who gets kidnapped or worse by passing torturers or a lustful wizard. This could all come across, of course, as distasteful to modern sensibilities, but there is such a strong sense of 'otherness' in Smith's stories, that whatever occurs in those worlds seems if not acceptable then natural and faithful to the environment. It's almost as if he wrote while under the influence of a mind-altering drug, and was merely recounting things he was seeing rather than making it all up.

I still have a story I wrote myself when I was in thrall to Smith's worlds. It's really cute in its woe and angst, its rotting towers, its endless Wastes (capitalisation of Terrible Deserts and Awful Crags *de rigeur*, of course), its revenant serpent people enslaved by a curse and so on. Smith was a great inspiration to me, until I went on to find writers like Michael Moorcock, Jack Vance and Tanith Lee, whose use of language was, while equally enthralling, much more suitable to modern writing. Still, I'll always have affection for the abominable monstrosities of the Lost Worlds. Zothique and its contemporaries are still bizarre and barely-frequented places, and tourism has not defiled them. Ideal for the discerning traveller.

I believe I wrote this piece for a magazine with an issue themed around Smith's work, or else an anthology of articles about him. Unfortunately, I can't trace the information now and the memory is lost.

The story I mention as being influenced by Smith is 'Curse of the Snake', which appears as a much revised and polished version in my 'Mythophidia' collection, through Immanion Press, 2008.

The Night Circus

Erin Morgenstern, Vintage 2012

and

Miss Peregrine's Home for Peculiar Children

Ransome Riggs, Quirk Books, 2011

Blog Post Review 2013

I was drawn most to *The Night Circus* and *Miss Peregrine's Home for Peculiar Children* by their titles. I was searching for some other book on Amazon at the time – forget what – and noticed these two, and on impulse bought them.

I really wanted to like *Miss Pegregrine*. As the start, it had echoes of *Submarine* by Joe Dunthorne, and I thought it might maintain this rather jaded, 'modern', reflection of children upon parents. That faded out. As for a magical reality aspect, this was well in force initially, and I was captivated by the artistic use of bizarre and often grotesque old photographs to illustrate the story, but again was not maintained in the same way.

The young protagonist, Jacob, ends up on a strange Welsh isle after the uncanny death of his grandfather, with the clue this island holds information about Grandpa's past and that he was a bit different to other people. What killed him for a start was rather unworldly. When Jacob first starts uncovering the mystery of his family, the story is great. What is not so great is that once the oohs and ahhs are delivered, it loses a lot of its initial weirdness.

The author had a great idea but squandered it. To me, he turned a really unusual and unsettling premise into a fairly pedestrian children's novel. Perhaps that was his intention, I don't know.

Riggs must have gone to great lengths to find the creepy ancient photos that illustrate the book – and they really are jarring and surreal. The children, when we first meet them through the eyes of the protagonist, are indeed peculiar and fascinating. Unfortunately, somewhere about half-way through the novel, it changes into another book. I found myself reading a 'jolly' children's adventure story, and the fact that the characters could be invisible, or float, or have other peculiarities, just made it like a WW2 period, British version of *X Men* – specifically aimed at young children. There are still some good ideas in the story – the boy in the bed being one of them – that genuinely is disturbing (won't say more because of spoilers), but I do feel the author lost his way with it. What began as an innovative and peculiar book became rather more stolid and predictable. And is clearly set up for a sequel.

By contrast, *The Night Circus* sustained itself far better; I enjoyed the novel from start to finish. It has a touch of *Something Wicked This Way Comes* (Ray Bradbury) about it, and also has similarities with the work of Steve Millhauser – who is the master of bizarre and macabre detail and who loves strange things like distinctly unusual circuses, automata, puppets and such like.

The Night Circus begins with two magicians who both have different ideas on the best way to train an apprentice in the art of magic. They agree to a challenge and decide to pit their trainees against each other in a game that will take years to complete, a challenge that only one of them will survive. Le Cirque des Reves (The Circus of Dreams) becomes the setting for his duel with Celia and Marco the unwitting pawns in the game with neither of them knowing the rules or even who their opponent is.

(From a review on Amazon)

The idea of two innocents being set up by cynical 'guardians' as magical rivals against each other, beginning when they are children, is compelling. We see them develop and eventually meet, with perhaps certain predictable consequences, but not entirely.

The flowering of the marvellous Circus, the rivals' 'battle ground', is also delicious, as are its inhabitants. The only detrimental comment I can make is while the story is a page turner, and the sets wondrous, I didn't really *care* much about the characters themselves. They were distant, somehow mechanical. But perhaps that was intentional. However, I will look out for this author's next book, whereas I don't really care what happens to Miss Peregrine's 'Famous Five', or whatever number it is, of rather ordinary peculiar children. Comparing it to *The Night Circus* is perhaps unfair, but in the latter novel we find delicacy, nuance, careful crafting and a skilled unfolding. *The Night Circus* can be enjoyed wholly by a far wider age range of readers.

'Miss Peregrine's Home for Peculiar Children' has already spawned two sequels and a graphic novel, and a big movie is in production, with a strong cast, and due for a spring 2016 release. I'll probably watch the movie but I'm not interested in the other novels.

A film of 'The Night Circus' is also mentioned on IMDB.com as 'in production', but with no further details. At the time of writing Erin Morgenstern has not published any further novels, although I hope to read more of her work in the future.

Her Fearful Symmetry

Audrey Niffenegger
Vintage, 2010

Review for Goodreads, October 2013

When Elspeth Noblin dies she leaves her beautiful flat overlooking Highgate Cemetery to her twin nieces, Julia and Valentina Poole, on the condition that their mother is never allowed to cross the threshold. But until the solicitor's letter falls through the door of their suburban American home, neither Julia nor Valentina knew their aunt existed. The twins hope that in London their own, separate, lives can finally begin but they have no idea that they've been summoned into a tangle of fraying lives, from the obsessive-compulsive crossword setter who lives above them, to their aunt's mysterious and elusive lover who lives below them and works in the cemetery itself.

As the twins unravel the secrets of their aunt, who doesn't seem quite ready to leave her flat, even after death, Niffenegger weaves together a delicious and deadly ghost story about love, loss and identity.

Cover Text to the novel

I have mixed feelings about this novel. On the one hand I read it quickly because I wanted to find out what happened, but on the other I found some of the characters' behaviour unbelievable. I just couldn't believe that the gruesome plan that's hatched in the last quarter or so of the book would be countenanced by its participants. If anything, it's sickening, and how any of them could see it as a feasible solution to a certain problem stretches credulity until it snaps. The only thing I could think was that the participants were selfish, stupid and/or weak to the extreme. I did find myself balking at reading the climax of that particular section. However, it wasn't as revolting as I feared it might be.

It's hard to warm to any of the characters, because all of them have traits that are irritating or they are plain stupid. While this does add a sense of realism – because who, in reality, is perfect? – the traits and stupidity did start getting on my nerves. But the setting of the novel is great - the old house overlooking Highgate Cemetery. I enjoyed learning about the history of Highgate and being given a glimpse of some of its fascinating stories. The writing is smooth and skilled, and the ghost of the novel is very different from the usual kind, being a strong and participating character in the story, not just a scary threat in the shadows.

I thought we were going to get a finish rather like *The Monkey's Paw*, and there is a short scene that seems to flag that that's the way it's heading, but then everything changes and the truly horrible becomes somewhat mundane. Still, it's an unusual tale, and I've not read anything like it, which is a good thing to be able to say about a book nowadays.

Slight spoiler and Warning for readers who don't want to come across cruelty to cats in a story – you might find part of this book extremely unpleasant. If I'd known of this section, I'd not have started reading the novel. Only curiosity about how the story ended stopped me putting it aside.

The House on Poultney Road
Based on a True Ghost Story
Stephanie Boddy
EBook only (Kindle)
Review Feb 2014

Sadly this is classic example of what happens when books aren't edited properly. The premise for the story is good enough for a supernatural tale – generations of a family living in a haunted house. That idea's been done to death, but – no matter – it still works for those of us who like our 'ghost fix'. And really, it's down to the individual writer to bring freshness to the formula; their own voice, and innovative detail.

This book just doesn't do these things. First, there are so many anachronisms I found it almost impossible to immerse myself in the story. The tale proper takes place back in the early 20th Century and the historical details didn't convince me. It's far too modern in tone and description. If the story had been set in the present day, it would have worked better, because the pitch of the language would have suited it. Also, the author wouldn't have had to bother herself with that pesky historical authenticity. As this is allegedly based on a true story, the anachronisms grate even more than they otherwise would. Plus the writing, while mostly grammatically correct, is rather clunky and pedestrian, littered with close repetitions of words.

The first chapter, set in the present, starts off fine, with the narrator managing to get inside her old family home, posing as a potential buyer, as it's up for sale. We get the author's honest impressions, plus memories of what she's been told about the place, and it sets up the story well.

Then in the next chapter we go back to 1923 and the start of the story in earnest. Great grand-parents of the narrator, Henry and Flo, buy the house in Poultney Road. The author claims this is based on a true family history, and the factual information she has of her relatives at this time is plentiful. It's only when she has to delve into conjecture, or 'novelises' the scant facts, that the anachronisms start creeping in.

Conversations between characters are voiced in a 21st Century idiom, and often involve modern ideas such as that of 'being depressed', and I'm not completely sure that anyone but the ultra-rich could have afforded an electric refrigerator or telephone in those days. Would British in-laws in the 1920s welcome home from hospital a new mother with balloons and banners all over the house? Would women even habitually have *gone* to hospital to give birth in those times?

After the birth of Flo and Henry's son, Richard, we are told of the mother's sleepless nights and how the baby's sleeping habits put a strain on the parents' relationship, as well as talk of 'second incomes', or rather the lack of one. At that time, in middle class families, women wouldn't have been expected to get a job. This all again seems far too modern – if they were well-off enough to own a fridge, wouldn't they have had a maid at least to attend to the child? And then, with Richard's growth to adulthood in the 1940s, I wasn't convinced that ordinary, middle class people 'in trade' would go out to dinner so much at restaurants during the WWII years and after – surely only for special occasions. The going out for meals simply seemed like a convenient way to get the parents out of the house, so Richard could be alone in it.

I think the main problem is that the reader isn't really sure what class the characters actually fall into, and in those times such distinctions were very important and informed how people lived day to day. A well-to-do middle class family in the very early 20th Century would have had at least one servant or maid, for example. And would a family at the lesser end of the financial scale be living in a property like Poultney Road? There are too many questions unanswered, too much incongruous detail, and to me glaring gaps in the history. '...*the economy was in a dire position, for various reasons.*' It seems like the writer didn't know the reasons, and the financial state of the country was glossed over as quickly as possible, even though that too would have influenced how people lived.

The author had the family ghost story handed down to her, (and a great story that is), but not all the *minutiae* that filled out the lives of those ancestors. She had to make that up to create the tale, and this is where the book falls down.

To be fair, the author does imply in her introduction that she was driven to write more by the need to record the family story than to be a novelist. But it is a shame, because the ghost story itself, following the generations, is a good one. The character Richard haunted by the death of a childhood friend, the presence of a mysterious man in black who might have been responsible for the child's death, and whose menace continues through time, the appearance of a genuinely spooky faceless female ghost in the house, all make for great narrative devices. If only the author had had a good editor to work with, the book could have been a lot better than it is. I could only read about half of it before I had to put it aside, irritated by the poor writing and the unlikely details – and by that I don't mean the ghosts, which strangely are the most believable of all.

This, to me, is an example of the downsides of eBook technology – barely edited, self-published works, or publishing companies that just churn out books regardless of the standard of writing, and who are no longer prepared to nurture new writers and help them with their craft. Books of this kind seem only to be treated as throwaway temporary products. It particularly pains me when you see a writer with promise, who with guidance could have crafted a very good novel, be let down in this way. Still, *The House on Poultney Road* picked up dozens of 5 star reviews on Kindle, which perhaps shows that the readership knows as much as the author about historical detail and skilled writing. That, or the author persuaded dozens of friends and family to review the book positively. This is not an uncommon occurrence on Amazon. The system can easily be 'played', which is grossly unfair on potential purchasers.

Hemlock Grove

Brian McGreevy

Reprint: Farrar Straus Giroux (July 2013)

Review: July 2014

An exhilarating reinvention of the gothic novel, inspired by the iconic characters of our greatest myths and nightmares.

The body of a young girl is found mangled and murdered in the woods of Hemlock Grove, Pennsylvania, in the shadow of the abandoned Godfrey Steel mill. A manhunt ensues – though the authorities aren't sure if it's a man they should be looking for.

Some suspect an escapee from the White Tower, a foreboding biotech facility owned by the Godfrey family – their personal fortune and the local economy having moved on from Pittsburgh steel – where, if rumours are true, biological experiments of the most unethical kind take place. Others turn to Peter Rumancek, a Gypsy trailer-trash kid who has told impressionable high school classmates that he's a werewolf. Or perhaps it's Roman, the son of the late JR Godfrey, who rules the adolescent social scene with the casual arrogance of a cold-blooded aristocrat, his superior status unquestioned despite his decidedly freakish sister, Shelley, whose monstrous medical conditions belie a sweet intelligence, and his otherworldly control freak of a mother, Olivia.

From the cover text of the book

If you've read any review of *Hemlock Grove* before this, you've no doubt found it has been slagged off a lot – not just the novel but also the TV show. The comment 'this is bad writing' or a variant thereof, crops up over and over. But just as it's possible to have bad writers in the world, it's equally possible to have bad readers.

When reading vintage literature, such as – for example – R D Blackmoore's *Lorna Doone,* (as I did recently), the language seems almost alien at first – the unfamiliar and complex style gets in the way of immersing yourself in the story. The only way to make friends with the prose is to slip into its rhythm, and then, like learning a foreign language, suddenly it clicks into place in your head and you 'get it'. The journey is smooth from then on. Brian McGreevy has been criticised for his use of language in *Hemlock Grove*, his strange sentence structure and quirky style. But in my opinion, this *is* a style and not bad writing. It's a brave style too. Once you fall into its rhythm its supposed infelicities don't jar.

As I began this review while I was still reading the book, I didn't know whether my opinions might change as I went deeper into the novel's territory, but this didn't happen. McGreevy kept me with him until the end. I'm a harsh reader to have, because I have little patience with bad or lazy writing. I've read a lot of it too, where I've almost thrown books down in disgust, but not once did I feel that way about McGreevy's story telling. In fact, I was intrigued and hooked.

This book is unashamedly modern Gothic – it plays with almost every trope of the genre, mixing the historic in with the new: the ancient, strange family dynasty living in a huge spooky mansion; the mad scientist doing bad things in a glass tower laboratory; the Frankenstein monster-like freak, who is simultaneously the family secret, yet *not* hidden away, being very much out in the world; the werewolf on the loose; a secret society of 'slayers'; the 'good' doctor caught up in the bizarre shenanigans and so on. I've spotted other nods towards Classic Gothic, some slipped in unobtrusively, which is obviously deliberate on the writer's part. The novel also has its more modern face, with its brutal murders, graphically depicted, and a perhaps unhealthy attachment to the description of giblets strewn about. I'm not a great fan of gore so had to steel myself to get through those sections.

The story is playful because it puts its cast of iconic Classic Horror characters smack bang in the middle of a 21st century world, and apparently – at first – another genre, because initially you might think you've landed in a Young Adult novel that's going to be full of annoying female teen characters worrying about boyfriends, and worse than that, *supernatural* boyfriends. But this novel is no *Twilight,* or indeed part of the plethora of weak supernatural romance YA 'literature' that's out there. Yes, the story does in some measure centre around high school, because Shelley, the giant freak, attends the local one, as does the werewolf and... well can't say too much because that would be a spoiler. (It's obvious from the start that Peter is a werewolf and Shelley is a freak.)

I really enjoyed this book as I enjoyed the camped-up, gory TV show. I've yet to see the second season, and as far as I know McGreevy has written no follow up. There are cliff-hangers aplenty in *Hemlock Grove,* which I hope one day get resolved. It's an intriguing story, both as a good (if experimental) read, but also could be of interest to students of creative writing because of its bold and unusual style.

At the time of writing, season two of 'Hemlock Grove' has been shown on Netflix and is available to purchase as Blu Ray or DVD. There is no novel tie-in. The third season, which will conclude the story, is due to be aired either later this year or in 2016. The filming has been completed.

The Best Till Last: Revisiting Manderley

Rebecca's Tale by Sally Beaumann,
The Other Rebecca by Maureen Freely
Mrs De Winter by Susan Hill.

Dreams of Dark Angels blog post, October 17th 2014

I've always been a fan of the story 'Rebecca', the novel written by Daphne Du Maurier, the Hitchcock film, and the later TV series, featuring the ever reptilian Charles Dance as Maxim (was never comfortable with that casting.) I knew that several novels had spun off from the original story over the years, but considered this a travesty, a calculating ploy by the publishing industry to claw in more bucks, rather than any honest attempt to continue the story with integrity. As it happens, I was wrong.

Only recently, and after a conversation at one of my 'writing and dining' evenings with friends Louise Coquio and Paula Wakefield, I decided to get hold of these novels, see for myself. The three of us are interested in the Gothic in fiction and all engaged in writing rather dark stories of our own at present. Our discussion of inspirations led us to Du Maurier and inevitably to *Rebecca*. Paula had read one of the 'sequels', *The Other Rebecca* by Maureen Freely and said that she'd enjoyed it and that it was written well. Lou had been given another of the three, *Rebecca's Tale* by Sally Beaumann, but hadn't yet read it. We took a look at Amazon and discovered the third book *Mrs De Winter* was by Susan Hill, one of my favourite ghost story writers. The next day, I ordered all of the books.

I will assume that anyone reading this will be familiar with the plot of the original novel, but if not, it can be found easily online. Here's a link so my following article will make sense. http://en.wikipedia.org/wiki/Rebecca_(novel) But if you haven't read that book, why not? Be aware though that spoilers concerning the original novel inevitably litter this article.

As Paula had recommended *The Other Rebecca* (2011) I read that first. It's a modern retelling of the story, with allusions to the original and includes quite clever twistings of that narrative. The Midwinters, as the original De Winters are renamed, are mostly monstrous. Mrs Danvers is not the cadaverous, looming creature we know from *Rebecca*, (sister in spirit clearly to the housekeeper of Hill House), but a more youthful, red-headed, while completely bonkers old friend of Rebecca's – Danny – who is still very much attached to the family after Rebecca's death and cares for her rather dislikeable children. (Maxim and Rebecca had no children in the original.) The story is told in the first person and the protagonist is a writer of minor importance struggling to make a career, while (like the original un-named second Mrs De Winter) being fraught with insecurities and anxieties. After her marriage to Maxim, she comes into a crazed nest of creative people and is at a loss at how to cope with them. They're cruel, sneering and condescending. Maxim's sister Beatrice, the stout rock of Du Maurier's novel, is still presented as strident but also scheming and untrustworthy. She's one of the more sympathetic characters, though. Big plot spoilers next, so skip to the next paragraph if you intend to read this book………………………..

There is a *Gone Girl* twist to *The Other Rebecca*, and the latter novel definitely came first. As with *Gone Girl*'s male lead, the selfish and priapic Maxim is being set up all the way through the story. The difference to the original *Rebecca* is: I didn't particularly care what happened to him. He's an unpleasant character, in turn whining and then callously aloof, bragging about his sexual conquests. Whatever his faults, I never saw the original Maxim as a whiner, blubbing into his wife's arms. He kept himself rigidly contained. If he'd ever had affairs, he would never have mentioned them, and certainly not to his wife. But this is a modern novel. The original Maxim would be an anachronism in it. As with the major characters in *Gone Girl*, Rebecca and Maxim are loathsome, spoilt, hedonistic and careless. Self-obsessed and narcissistic creative souls, who happened to have great talent, despite their failings. The bone of contention between them was always their work. (Still part of the spoiler: a neat detail is Danny 'getting messages' from Rebecca, which you imagine are lies or delusions, rather than true psychic communication, but of course... they're actually real, and Rebecca orchestrates everything from afar.)

But despite the nature of the characters, or perhaps because of it, the author pulls it off. While I did find the over-extended Midwinter family and its inter-relationships hard to follow, I suspect this is deliberate, since the protagonist herself can't keep track of the milling relatives either. Sometimes the story is too inscrutable and I found myself rereading parts to see if I'd missed something. Maybe a second read through is required to 'get' everything. Danny, like Mrs Danvers, is still obsessed with Rebecca, who was a famous poet, and is engaged in collating her correspondence in order to write a book. She keeps Rebecca's workroom as a shrine. In this story, it isn't the dead woman's silky negligees that are the fetishes, but her comfy slippers under the desk, the ash trays, the little clay models her children made. Danny isn't a reliable biographer. She has an agenda, and while there's no indication she has a murderous hatred towards and jealousy of the protagonist, she does see this woman as an instrument to help her achieve her aims. This is a world of novelists, tabloid journalism seeking thrills, and professional rivalry.

Manderley, the De Winter house, was a major character in *Rebecca*, but Beckfield, the house in *The Other Rebecca* plays no great part. It's Bea's house. Maxim and his wife live in a large cottage in the grounds. Strangely, though, when the new wife arrives at Beckfield to attend a sprawling garden party, full of twittering authors, artists and poets, the first thing Danny says to her is: 'Welcome to Manderley.' A knowing aside, as if the book *Rebecca* exists in that world and Danny is aware of the peculiar similarities between her life and the novel.

Apart from borrowing the central idea and skeletons of the characters from Du Maurier, Freely has written a book unconnected with the original. But I didn't dislike it, read it quickly, and appreciated the strength and skill of the writing, although even as I'm writing up this review can't remember the end. It's not a book I'd want to read twice.

I wanted to save Susan Hill's *Mrs De Winter* (1993) till last, as I like her writing so much and considered the Beaumann novel might be lightweight, as I associated her work with 'women's romantic novels', a sort I don't like to read. (Happily, I was later proved wrong on that count.) But I just couldn't resist picking up *Mrs De Winter* after the Freely, probably because I wanted to snuggle into writing I knew I'd really enjoy. And I'm glad I did because chronologically (in the ongoing story) this is the book that should be read after *Rebecca*. Beaumann's carries on from Hill's.

Hill keeps the voice of the original novel and this is truly a sequel. Maxim and his wife are still in exile at the start, living in posh hotels, with few belongings, wandering about Europe, settling for a few months here and there. Ten years have passed. They have a found a quiet space between them, where it's comfortable for them to live, after the traumas of the past and their flight from England at the end of *Rebecca*. But even so, right from the start we're made aware that Mrs De Winter can't suppress the memory that her husband killed Rebecca. He has a murderer's hands. Much as the mild, damaged man she cares for now seems removed from the person who could commit such a crime of passion – he still did it. His wife also misses her home country immensely. When they receive a call from Giles, Beatrice's husband, to tell them she has died from a stroke, Mrs De Winter's first thought is that they must return home for the funeral. Maxim stalls, clearly terrified of the prospect. But duty wins through and they return. Manderley is long gone, and is never mentioned by the family. Mrs De Winter doesn't know if it's still in ruins, has been restored, or whether the land has been bought up and modern houses built on it. We never find out. But once she's back on English soil, she knows she can't bear to leave it again, and wonders how she can persuade Maxim to let them settle there. The past is done. There's nothing left to haunt them, no reason not to come back. (Slight spoilers follow but nothing major.)

But of course, the central conflict of the story is that there is a reason to stay away. A simmering desire for vengeance still burns in the hearts of those who most loved Rebecca – or were obsessed by her. The first sign of trouble is a wreath left on Beatrice's grave, which Mrs De Winter stumbles upon after the funeral. Perfect white flowers in dark green foliage, and a card signed with the single letter R, in Rebecca's distinctive curling script. This must be a cruel joke. Mrs De Winter eventually takes the card and hides it.

Suppressing this information, coupled with a visit to Maxim's former estate manager, Frank Crawley's new home in Scotland, plus the sheer bewitching glamour of the British countryside, enables Mrs De Winter to convince Maxim they can come home at last. On a final motoring tour of England before they return abroad, they come across the house Cobett's Brake, a vision of beauty and old England. Not immense as Manderley was, but a comfortable, sagging manor house in the heart of the countryside. Both fall in love with the place, even though Maxim is clearly nervous of admitting that to himself, and for a while he stalls and insists they return to Europe. Mrs De Winter simmers with resentment and anger, but it's not in her nature to shout and stamp her foot about it. While touring Italy, she has a peculiar experience when Manderley housekeeper Mrs Danvers' voice returns to her, whispering in her ear, savaging her self-confidence. But again, she remains silent. And when on her birthday, Maxim presents her with the information that Cobett's Brake is now hers, (he has secretly negotiated its purchase with Crawley), she feels her life is to begin anew. And so it does for some time. She and Maxim enjoy an idyllic few months in their new home, which is as far from Manderley as it's possible to get. It's like a mother to Mrs De Winter. She feels protected there.

But then, on a visit to London to visit a gynaecologist, (she hopes to have children), she bumps by chance into Rebecca's louche cousin, Jack Favell. He looks as if he's been living on the street, and because Mrs De Winter lacks the strength of character to tell him where to go, or indeed call the police when he follows her into a hotel, she ends up having tea with him, giving him money, hoping this will be enough to get rid of him. As if! Then, on her return home, the newspaper clippings of Rebecca's death start to arrive. And so begins the build up to the storm that will engulf Mrs De Winter and her world. As her strength wanes, Mrs Danvers comes back into her life, turning up at the house, apparently on a polite social call, as she's been engaged as companion to an old lady in the area. As terrified of and intimidated by this dour female as she ever was, Mrs De Winter keeps Mrs Danvers' visit and proximity secret from Maxim, and limply allows Danvers to manipulate her. She even accepts an invitation to tea at Danvers' place of employment. Whatever spurts of strength she experiences are literally like damp squibs, sputtering a bit but failing to explode.

As the secrets build up, and the storm clouds build, and Mrs De Winter attempts to hang on to control of her life and protect Maxim from the past, we know that her world will inevitably tumble about her. We knew that from page one, really.

The spare version of the plot above makes the story sound more exciting than it is. *Mrs De Winter* is a very slow-moving book. The De Winters don't get to Cobett's Brake until two thirds of the way through the novel, and it's only then, really, that the story gets going. Until that point, there are endless – if beautiful – descriptions of countryside, houses, nature and weather.

Endless self-pity. Too much of all that, and not enough story. But I thought then, and still do, that this perhaps was intended, to make the novel 'literary' rather than 'popular' – the exciting elements are played down. I got fed up of Mrs De Winter telling me she'd found new strength, only to find that no, she hadn't. She was as limp as ever and remained so throughout. Rebecca would have had none of the nonsense her successor passively subjects herself to. She'd have had Favell and Danvers out of her home with a gun pointed at their heads the moment they appeared. But still, the fact remains that Maxim was guilty of murder, however much he was pushed to it. And he *did* get away with it.

I did enjoy the book but not as much as I'd hoped. On the cover, one of the gushing blurbs called it a 'ghost story', so I was hoping for one of Hill's superb, eerie tales with more than a hint of the supernatural. But the ghosts in *Mrs De Winter* remain firmly in people's minds. That didn't disappoint me so much, though, as the fact the story was turgid, too slow, too full of hand wringing and sighs. It would have been more satisfying for me if Mrs De Winter had in fact grown up, grabbed her demons by the throat and turned the tables on them. However, the voice of the narrator is perfect, and it's a convincing sequel to Du Maurier's original. This book was my second favourite of the three.

But first prize must go to Sally Beaumann's *Rebecca's Tale* (2001). Again, she keeps the voice of the original well, in terms of time and place, but the first narrator, in a novel of four parts, is the aged Colonel Julyan, who presided over Rebecca's inquest. He's always had his suspicions about what truly happened, but the mistake that Favell made, and perhaps readers too, is that he didn't keep his suspicions quiet in order to protect Maxim and his family name, as was implied. He kept his silence in order to protect Rebecca, as he'd been very fond of her. The novel starts with him reminiscing over the past, because an upstart author wants to write yet another book about the Manderley mystery, which has become folklore in its part of the world. Julyan recollects his long relationship with the De Winter family, and I loved his description of being a boy, playing at the great old house. His portraits of the terrifying De Winter matriarch, (Maxim's grandmother), the kind but wilting Virginia (his mother) and her glorious sisters, and of Bea and Maxim as children, are wonderful. The story draws you right in from the start because what happened to Rebecca was wholly tied up with the way the De Winters were, an ancient family going back eight hundred years. There's more than a whiff of authors like P G Wodehouse and Evelyn Waugh, in the light, acerbic wit of the writing. This is nowhere near a 'women's romantic novel'.

I was surprised – and pleased – to find *Rebecca's Tale* keeps to the 'canon' found in Hill's' – i.e. what happened to the De Winters when they returned to England, or at least as much of that as Julyan and other major characters can possibly know – which is only the bare facts. Still, this novel carries on neatly from Hill's, and it seems to me that Beaumann must have known of that book and kept to the same story. Or the similarities are just uncanny coincidences…

Part two of the story is told by Terence Grey, the writer who's in Kerrith investigating the story of Rebecca. Grey is a complex character, with secrets and tragedies of his own. His interest in the old story lurches towards obsession, dangerously so. Through Grey we meet some of the other characters from *Rebecca* and hear their version of events – such as the cousin Jack Favell, Frith the erstwhile butler of Manderley, and other colourful Kerrith characters. The truth about Rebecca, it seems, is more convoluted than everyone thought. Her own history is revealed in tantalising glimpses – the girl she'd once been and the woman she became, who was mistress of Manderley. The reader begins to learn about her heritage. While Grey investigates, an anonymous individual is sending notebooks of Rebecca's to Colonel Julyan, and is also perhaps the same person who leaves a wreath at Rebecca's old boathouse cottage, and sends a piece of her jewellery to Favell. Mysteries mount, and I couldn't turn the pages fast enough!

Part three is Rebecca's own tale, as found in the second notebook sent to Julyan. But we know already that Rebecca is often a minx. Is her testimony reliable? Whether this is true or not, it's riveting to read. A free spirit, Rebecca was born ahead of her time, totally unsuited to a woman's life in the early part of the 20th century. She suffered for her difference, as she was rarely understood. And the tragic way she narrates her story to an unborn child she believes she is carrying is moving while being unsentimental. Naturally, Rebecca's tale is cut short by her own death. Many threads are left dangling.

Part four is related by Ellie, Colonel Julyan's daughter. Hers is a strong, true voice, but even she has her obsession with Rebecca, seeing in the dead woman a promising template for female emancipation at a time in history when women were fighting for their rights, and most men still regarded them as mistresses, mothers or domestics. Ellie's is undoubtedly the most political account, but she is also a vibrant, convincing character with her own desires and dreams. Ellie uncovers more mysteries, and in one case solves one, while simultaneously growing as a person. During her account, the narrative never falters. All four narrators, each with their distinctive voice, carry the story along at a good pace, but it is still deep and ponderous – and I don't mean that in a bad way. This is not a short or shallow book by any means.

Most, but not all, the threads finally weave together and the reader is left to make up their own mind. You don't feel in any way short-changed by that, though. What Beaumann has done is create a convincing account, including the difficulty of discovering historical truths, when the main protagonists are dead. Some truth died with them. Rebecca affected everyone she met, often dramatically. She is perhaps all the things everyone ever thought her to be, and more, a girl who fought to survive throughout a difficult childhood and adolescence, who set her will at making an adult life for herself, to her liking. But she is always human, believable. Her gift to Ellie is revealed at the end of book, perhaps far different from what you expect all the way through. I loved that. My favourite book of those I've read over the past few years is *The Little Stranger* by Sarah Waters, but Sally Beaumann's *Rebecca's Tale* will now be stored on the same shelf.

Of these three Rebecca novels only the Hill and the Beaumann can be seen as continuations of the story. In fact, with the original they effectively make up a trilogy. And yes, there could be more to tell, should some other writer be urged to take up the tale. The Freely is entirely separate, while still quite an interesting read. But it's not connected with the beguiling, mysterious Rebecca as we know her.

On My Own Work

A Resonance of Symbols:
Sign for the Sacred

Article for Inception fan club magazine
17th December 1992

It has seemed to me that certain of my books go in 'sets'. The Wraeththu books, obviously, go together, as do *The Monstrous Regiment* and *Aleph*, not just for the fact that they share worlds, but because they encapsulate a part of my writing history. Wraeththu was written by The Eager Innocent, bursting with ideas. The books were a magical initiation for me into my craft; I 'felt' them, rather than simply wrote them. *The Monstrous Regiment,* however, was penned by a person who still wanted to be innocent, but wasn't and *Aleph*, following on from that, by a writer reconciled to the fact that for her, Wraeththu would always stand out in her mind as the work that was 'easy', and that not all her writing would burst forth like that. This was where the hard work started. The incense-shrouded ritual was over; it would be necessary to live and work in the real world for a while.

Hermetech and *Burying the Shadow* also seem to go together for me. Both were complex stories, and in some ways represented a groomed style rather than an abandoned one, typified by the Wraeththu books. These were books in which I explored themes and concepts. *Sign for the Sacred*, however, will stand up on its own. It is a crossroads book, leading to what I feel will be a more self-assured and stylised piece of work, *Calenture*.

I have had a very mixed bag of reactions to 'Sacred', and this before the book has even been published! However, in the light of some observations and queries, I feel that I should talk about the book for Inception magazine. I would like to discuss my intentions in writing this book, and to illustrate how the end result was not achieved accidentally, but deliberately.

Steve Jeffery wrote to me with the comment, *"...there seem to be several books here, in different styles almost, rather than separate threads to a novel."* Steve's favourite 'thread' was the story of Lucien Earthlight, which I saw as the backbone of the book, the steady core to the world of Gleberune itself. Although Lucien encounters surreality in his life, and his travels, for the most part his story is 'straight'. He attempts to move through the world from A to B, trying to understand what has happened to him, generally convinced there is a logical explanation to everything. He is a seeker, and the object of his search, and desire, is Resenence Jeopardy, a man of masks.

Jeopardy is many different things to different people: charlatan or magus especially. Lucien wants to believe he is either one of these; he cannot cope with the idea that Jeopardy might be both.

However, as in real life, people's perceptions of the world create their own brand of reality. There are others in the story who can quite happily accept the more bizarre aspects of Jeopardy's persona. For them, life is a magical journey, and nothing has to be explained, simply accepted.

Cleo Sinister, a kooky character, invites the bizarre and peculiar into her life and therefore experiences them. Often, her adventures border on farce. What could be truly sinister are rendered laughable; that is Cleo's effect on the proceedings. She is a restless, irreverent individual; for her the light of life is a kaleidoscope, constantly moving. Therefore, the shadows are only glimpsed briefly.

All too often, a fantasy book contains only one perception of the world in which it is set. Generally, this is undoubtedly essential for the story. In 'Sacred', however, I wanted to bend the rules. Lucien Earthlight has a life of tragedy and confusion, and consequently follows the path he has hewn for himself. If Lucien had been the one to experience the unusual habits of the Sisters of True Valiance, the episode would indeed have been darker and more unsettling, but that was Cleo's adventure, and for her it was simply absurd. However, the actions of those particular Sisters are intended to magnify the conceptions (or misconceptions) of the fanatically religious. When I come across the strictures such people place upon themselves in an attempt to seek spirituality I see it as pathetic, laughable and perverse. The Sisters of True Valiance are these perverse tendencies condensed, taken to extreme. It is easy to laugh until you think that there are people in this world who hold similar beliefs: the Brides of Christ, for example, who have taken vows of purity and celibacy, yet have symbolically married themselves to a god. Marriage implies to conjunction of flesh; what are the secret fantasies of the Brides when they are alone in their cold beds?

The episode in the Sisters' fane was not intended to be a comment upon sexual masochism and chivalry, but simply a report of the Sisters' belief system, seen through Cleo's eyes. Before Cleo opened the door to the chapel, what was ensuing inside might have been gravid with spiritual meaning. It was only her irreverent eyes that smacked the ritual straight into the ridiculous. The scene could have been written many ways, but its tone was directed by its protagonist; Cleo.

Other 'cartoon-like' characters, such as the two Jeopardites encountered by Delilah Latterkin, and the vampire, Lord Pliance, are again perhaps rather cruel parodies of certain types I have encountered in my own life. First, the Jeopardites, Nebuline Midnoon and Inshave Macassar. These are the personification of those who are obsessed with the romantic ideas of death and dissolution. To negate the celebration of life is, to me, not just sad and pathetic but risible. When dead, which seems to be the desired object of these people's fantasies, the supposed romanticism and decadence of espousing these ideals can no longer be experienced and enjoyed. Therefore, it can only be a shallow obsession, a posture. The beauty of being a pale and bloodless corpse laid out on a velvet bed, lilies laid on a motionless white breast, is pointless if you're not there to appreciate yourself, surely? Therefore, act it out, wear the make-up of the corpse and shroud yourself in grave-cloth. Fake death, but cheat it! Essentially it's a celebration of life, I suppose, but the lack of humour, the absence of an awareness of self-parody, strips the posture of any true meaning.

Similarly, Lord Pliance typifies my opinions of those obsessed with vampires. To me, the vampire is a sexual motif, more to do with the little death of orgasm than the eternal death of, well, death. The traditional vampires were hideous creatures, far from the suave, erotic creations that exemplify the breed nowadays in the pages of literature and in movies. Lord Pliance acts out his required role; aristocratic, predatory, murderous. Yet he himself is not shy of self-parody. He is aware of what he is. As he says to Delilah, *"Were I in your position, travelling a wild and desperate land such as this, I would hurry past any dark, forbidding residences such as Castle Pliance. What did you expect to find in this awful place? I am a vampire. You should have recognised my setting."*

Nebuline and Inshave, of course, take him very seriously. Delilah suspects they are lying in their beds waiting for the vampire's deadly kiss, and she is undoubtedly correct, but it is to innocent Delilah that Lord Pliance is drawn, the very person who is immune to his advances. That, I suspect, is the fate of all those who court the vampire, all those who espouse the cloak, the black, the white face, the red lips. While they lie there in their finery waiting for the shadow of a bat against the bedroom wall, the vampire is despoiling and ravaging an ignorant innocent next door, who probably didn't even believe in him. To a vampire, his fans would not be tender morsels, being too easy, too desperate to be like him. Hardly forbidden fruit. If only he could hear them laughing at themselves, he might be more interested.... still.

The religion of Ixmarity, which is the backdrop to the book, is not based upon any one particular belief system in existence in our world, but is simply present as the masked face of organised religion. It is not outrightly perverse, but many of its adherents bend its creeds to their own perversions, as in the case of Wilfish Implexion, the ecclesiarch bent on Jeopardy's destruction (or rape, which is nearer the truth of the matter). Ultimately, Implexion cannot be true to his own desires – which is to become a follower of Jeopardy, to be near him – for to give in to that secret longing, would be to destroy the fascination of denial, the enjoyment of frustration and bitterness. Implexion torments himself so much with his longings, he denies himself even the pleasure of fantasising about them. He too creates his own image of Jeopardy, and in achieving what he perceives as Jeopardy's murder, can no longer live, for all that sustained his life, made it worth living, has been consumed, used up, destroyed.

Steve's final comments about 'Sacred' were, *"Trajan and Delilah, and the way they picked up the others on the way in their quest for Resenence, reminded me of the Wizard of Oz story – a heart, a brain, a child, a cure for madness..."*

In some ways, Resenence Jeopardy *is* like the Wizard of Oz; others have created his image, while he recreates himself continually. The travellers, the questers, are not looking for Resenence Jeopardy himself, but simply their image of him, their desire of what he should be. At the same time, Trajan the madman, Delilah the innocent child, Cleo the heartless femme fatale, (who holds the cure to madness in her bag of poisons), Dauntless the doomed Quixotic knight, Lucien the abandoned lover, Pliance the predator, Nebuline and Inshave the mincing grotesques, are all aspects of Jeopardy himself. They have created him; he has created them. He draws them to him, only to reject them all and dream up a new persona for himself. Only Lucien is given a second chance to follow him, and one day Lucien will be unable to resist taking that offer up, for Jeopardy is his destiny, his geas – inescapable – even though Lucien is bright enough to be aware of the fact that the man he loves exists only in his fantasies, a man who looks like Resenence Jeopardy.

Like the Wraeththu books, *Sign for the Sacred* is a work of initiation, but in achieving the next level of existence, it is necessary to embrace a cosmic humour as well as enter Chapel Perilous. 'Sacred' is, as I said, a cross-roads book, but it should be read at more than face value. It is a book of many levels, and contains many secrets, of and by myself, and others.

The world is an infinity of different realities. Some people live in a kind of fairyland, and it is real to them. They create their own myths and live them. Others living in a humdrum, boring world and it never changes.... There is no magic in their lives, no possible space for it. But, despite these different views, everyone lives in the same world. Fairies and magic exist for one person but not for another. Both are right, because they have created their world that way.

Blocked

Prophecy APA contribution June 1998

A while ago a friend of mine, Anne Gay, asked me to contribute an article for her web site 'Fifth Column'. She asked for a rant about the depravities of the publishing industry. That's easy. Most writers do that nowadays; it comes with the job. But then, I thought again, and decided that I didn't so much want to rant about that, which makes writing difficult enough, but tackle a more fundamental problem that comes from within writers themselves: when writing becomes almost impossible. Writer's block. The muse takes a hike and we have no music inside us. We feel we have nothing to say. It's the most crippling sensation we can experience in our work. Anne, however, said she really would prefer me to dish the dirt on the publishing world, (as it was more appropriate for her site at the time), so I did that for her instead. But my initial thoughts stayed with me, so I thought I'd write them up for Prophecy. Seeing as quite a few Prophets are also writers, it seemed an appropriate place to do it.

I don't know if it's the same for every author, but when I was a child, writing little stories to amuse myself, and then later as a teenager, churning out purple prose in the name of fantasy, the creative process was easy. I looked forward to the times when I could write and filled dozens of exercise books with my meanderings. Even my first finished book – and its sequels – poured out of my head in a ceaseless stream, (although I look upon my first three books as one book.) Then something happened and suddenly, or perhaps it was gradually, writing became more difficult.

Writing is still what I want to do more than anything, which is why I puzzle over the fact that sometimes it seems the hardest thing to do.

Before any of my work was published, I wrote with innocence. What I produced was for myself alone, or any friends with whom I felt comfortable enough to reveal my stories. I also wrote with passion, for its own sake. If anyone should criticise what I did, why should it matter? As long as I was satisfied, everything was OK. This is not, however, a complaint about critics or criticism. The stripping away of ignorance that accompanies the shock of having your work analysed must certainly contribute to the problem, but I don't believe it's the problem's foundation.

The first consequence of having work reviewed, or receiving readers' letters, is that you become aware of an audience. Your work is no longer private, and people are free to interpret what you've written in whatever way they choose. But I still think that is part of the post-writing scenario. When you're actually writing, you forget about that audience. It is you and the book alone. Awareness of an audience is not the crux of the problem.

Then you have the dilemma of writing material that will sell. I'm not talking about mega-sales in shops, but actually getting a publisher excited enough about one of your ideas to want to buy it. The situation has certainly changed since I was first signed up. It seems reasonable that publishers are cautious about first novels and want to see a sizeable chunk of a book before they'll commit themselves. But now this caution also applies to books that come from seasoned writers, who can be trusted, more or less, to do the job they promise. 'So what?' you might say. If you're going to write the book anyway, why not rattle off a hundred or so pages before getting an agent to hawk it around? OK, nobody might take it up, and that's a risk if writing is your sole source of income. Could it be this uncertainty that causes writer's block? I don't think so. I know writers who have not yet sold a novel, and they also experience the black wave of block.

I can remember that when I first began writing, I literally

couldn't stop. If my life, the roof over my head, or my next meal had depended on me producing words, I wouldn't have found those responsibilities an impediment to creativity. It might be easy to say that now, and I have no way of testing it, but from what I can feel and remember, I know that if someone had said to me, when I was about eighteen, "write! Your life depends on it!" I would have thought, "Wow, what an easy way to save my life." I wrote obsessively, sneakily bashing out a few pages at work when the boss wasn't looking, snatching half an hour at my battered old typewriter before I got ready to go out in the evening. Now, if I don't have a clear run at it, i.e. less than a whole afternoon or evening, I think "that's not enough time. I won't be able to get into it."

Why? Why this effort now? I don't believe that getting older has caused me to slow down. If anything, I've got more to write about. I have lots of experience, and am a far better writer than I was at eighteen.

These thoughts led me to a certain conclusion, but it's taken me a long time to realise it. I believe the creative process is stultified by the very fact that the more you write, the more skilled you become. This might sound contradictory, but I hope I can explain. You'll have to bear with me, because this realisation came to me very late at night, while I lay awake in bed fretting about not working the day before.

When you write your first book or story, you are heading off into new territory. You have no identical previous experiences to compare it with. That first book/story might not sell, and you'll plunge into the next, hoping it will, but still the mechanism I'm talking about does not come into play. Once you are published, you think, perhaps wrongly, that your work has become valid. Whatever you did before just wasn't the real thing. Therefore, the next thing you write has to be compared with the first, not just by you, but everyone who reads it. You have set a standard, which you have to excel. This breeds only one thing: terror. Your innocence has been violated.

You might not even realise you're afraid. You've got a strong synopsis and are itching to get writing it. Your head is full of ideas. Characters are bursting for release from your mind. Then you actually get to your computer, typewriter, pen and notepad, or whatever, and quite often the first chapter or opening paragraph will dutifully empty itself from your imagination onto the page. Then that hideous something happens. You think you can't do it. You don't necessarily feel afraid even then: you feel despair.

Looked at dispassionately, this is ridiculous. You are a writer, it's what you do – you might have even written over a dozen novels before. You know the ropes, about structure and pace and all the other technicalities that can be the downfall of the novice. You know how to play with words and language. You have a story in your head, you *know* it, so why on earth can't you write it?

I cannot count the times I've sat at my computer, head in hands, staring at the screen, totally unable to write anything that seems remotely interesting or fresh. What I am doing, of course, is unconsciously comparing all that I've done before with what I'm trying to do now. What if I can't do it again? What if it's not as good? But it's not just the past that bugs me. I worry about the future too. *Oh God, I can't work today. I won't reach the deadline, and if I don't get my advance in time, I won't be able to pay those bills. This block might go on for weeks. What if I can't write for months?*

None of these horrors have happened yet, so why do I torture myself about them?

Creativity should spring forth unimpeded by the burden of memory or assumption. It should be spontaneous, and I do believe it can be, but first you have to dispel the obsession of living in the past and the future. When you write, I think you have to train yourself to exist solely in the present moment, so that anxieties, past or future, cannot intrude.

Every one of us wants to be successful in life, and to hang on to that success once we've got it. But we are immobilised by the fear of losing it, or not even attaining it in the first place. We look at other writers, and think they have achieved more than we have, or they write so much better than we do, how can we ever hope to compete? But everything we might think about in those dark moments comes from the past or the future. We can't possibly know what's happening to other writers at that precise moment we're trying to work, because we're stuck in our houses, head in hands. We *remember* what we know about them or *imagine* what might happen in days to come.

All our previous work exists in the past. It was written by who we were then, and now we're different. We've had thousands of new experiences that have changed us. Why then can't we write from the present moment and recapture that heady feeling of freedom that came with writing as a child or a teenager? Because that was what it was like back then, certainly for me. I didn't care about what I'd written before, whether it was a year ago or the previous day. I didn't care what I'd be writing tomorrow. I wrote entirely in the present. I didn't make comparisons, either with my earlier work, or other people's. I wrote what I felt. I was not afraid of being unable to write.

To me, it's a vicious circle. Fear of not being able to write makes us unable to write, and if we're unable to write, we become even more afraid. Even the act of remembering how easy it once was to write, and comparing it to the present, generates more fear. Our whole identity is wrapped up in being a writer. If we fail, we fail as people, not just as writers. So that is what I realised in bed that night; writer's block is terror. The fear is not a consequence, but a cause, and bizarrely enough it stems from becoming more skilled at what you do. I often say to new writers, who ask me for advice, "Don't worry about the quality of your first drafts. Just write. Get it out. Then you can go back and tweak and polish." Unfortunately, I cannot practise what I preach, although I am working on it.

Happily, writer's block rarely paralyses me for too long.

Some days, writing is easy. I think: how could I ever find this difficult? I have yet to work out how the fear gets a grip on certain days and not on others. Could it be down to natural body and mood rhythms, the hormonal cycle or simply what I ate and drank the day before? If I had the answer to that, I'm sure I could make a fortune! I've given up trying to fight the black wave and when it strikes now, just try to accept it as temporary and not torture myself with guilt about not working.

From Wraeththu to Grigori:
the Sorcerer's Path

Web site post, 27th January, 1999

Many people have asked me, "are you going to do any more Wraeththu books, and if so, when?" Admittedly, most of these requests do come from the States, where the majority of readers think the Grigori trilogy is actually the follow-up to the Wraeththu series, because nothing else of mine has yet been published over there. However, this question does come from other readers too, who have read everything I've written in between, but who still think the Wraeththu books are my best work.

You can imagine that this is quite demoralising for a writer. I'm fifteen years older than I was when I explored the world of Pellaz and Cal, and therefore fifteen years wiser and fifteen years more skilled. Has nothing I've written since Wraeththu been as good as that? I beg to differ, but I have thought about this matter and have come up with some answers as to why people are so fond of those initial and, it has to be said, quite flawed works.

The Wraeththu had lived inside my head for eight years before I even began work on writing the books. They first made themselves known to me in 1977. I was stuck in a job I hated and with a partner who was no good for me. My only escape was into a world of fantasy, and there I lived most of the time. Whenever I walked to work, I was there. Whenever I was doing some mundane task during the day, I was there. This went on for years, even after I'd changed jobs several times, got rid of the problematical partner, and owned my own house. I wrote poems about the hermaphroditic beings I'd dreamed up. I made up stories in my head, and even noted some of them down, although it wasn't until 1985 that I made a major decision concerning my fantasies. I was at work, at a computer terminal, bored almost to death, looking at the clock every thirty seconds, and wishing my life away. All I lived for was the time to go home. I was twenty-seven, looking at thirty down a long straight road, and basically I was scared. Was this how my life was going to be forever? No. It was not. It *mustn't* be.

That afternoon, I cleared the screen I was working on, and wrote what turned out to be the first paragraph of *Enchantments of Flesh and Spirit*. I won't go into the story about the incredible luck I had, which meant my first novel was accepted by the first publisher I sent it to. It's been told too many times. What I want to talk about is the way I felt when I wrote those first three books and what shaped them.

I had lived with those stories for so long that by the time I came to write them down in a coherent form, they just poured out in an unending stream. Not so now, but back then, writing was as unconscious to me as breathing. I had no awareness of an audience, I was writing for myself. I wanted to sell the book, yes, but would have written it even if publication hadn't been an option. I knew that what I was writing was in many ways controversial, and certainly ground-breaking in terms of SF and fantasy, where sex was still rather an end of scene fade-out and differences in sexual orientation generally unmentionable. I wasn't sure any publisher would take it. The people I saw around me in the Goth scene of that time, in the night clubs and the bands, inspired the characters in the books. People who were androgynous and slinky. People who were beautiful, and that didn't necessarily mean they all looked like super-models or movie stars. The beauty came from within, from being vibrant, from being peacocks. They flirted with the symbols of death and vampirism, but early Goths were never melancholy or po-faced. They were mischievous iconoclasts. These creatures were my muses. I wrote with passion, yet with innocence, ignorant of the publishing world and all the horrors that were waiting for me there. I knew nothing about marketing, sales figures, critics, or even an audience. I felt I was doing what the universe meant me to do.

I think that the innocence and passion somehow insinuated themselves between the words, so that the books existed on different levels. It might sound egotistical, but I'm sure some weird magic within the prose touched certain people who read it. There was no mechanical aspect to what I did; it was purely emotional and spiritual. It was my vision, and I wanted to share it at any cost. I was writing the books I'd always wanted to read, and there were people out there who were similar to me, who wanted to read those books too.

Looking back now, I can see the technical faults within the Wraeththu books, and parts of book one make me writhe and cringe in embarrassment. Some sections of *Enchantments* were incredibly cheesy and unlikely, and, as my critics gleefully pointed out at the time, there was hardly a plot to speak of. The grammar was dodgy too. Yet despite these flaws, the book worked in some strange way, and many readers loved it. Not so the publishers. *Enchantments* did fairly well, and I naively believed I was on the path to fame and fortune, but as so often happens, the second and third books, (which were technically far superior to the first), were not given the same fanfare at publication time. Their distribution to the trade was bad too, so they didn't sell nearly as well. Perhaps also the hard-core SF and fantasy readership weren't ready for my material, and although advance publicity might have intrigued them enough to buy the first book, they were uncomfortable with the subject matter and didn't want to read the rest of the trilogy. All these factors meant that the three synopses I had worked out for a further trilogy of Wraeththu books were rejected. If I was serious about writing as a career, I had no choice but to do something different.

I cannot describe how painful this was for me. I loved the Wraeththu world, and still wanted to live in it through my writing. Being told I could not do this was like standing on the threshold of a paradise garden and having the gate slammed shut in my face. I'd fondly believed I could follow in the footsteps of the many writers who had written whole series of books about their invented worlds. Also, I had never planned to appeal simply to a SF and fantasy audience. I hadn't wanted to end up in the ghetto of a genre, but that was what had happened.

One thing that writing had given me was freedom, for I was now only working in a day job part-time. I couldn't give up this freedom, because employment to me was slow death. So, I compromised, and *The Monstrous Regiment* was the result. It's not among the best of my novels, and was hell to write, because it did not come from the same pool of inspiration as Wraeththu had. It was a struggle, and was subsequently panned with delight by the critics. The sequel, *Aleph*, is a far better piece of work, but was virtually invisible in the shops, owing to the fact it was only ever published in trade paperback form, (a new larger format, which at first wasn't too popular), and had no promotion at all. As far as the publishing world was concerned, I had earned a reputation, 'She Who Does Not Sell', and that is a hard reputation to shake off.

Fortunately, I was then taken on by Headline and wrote four books I still feel proud of: *Hermetech*, *Burying the Shadow*, *Sign for the Sacred* and *Calenture*. However, in my quest for literary credibility, I think my work became increasingly impenetrable. I liked what I was writing, but I'd closed in on myself. *Sign for the Sacred* and *Calenture* were bloodletting exercises, in which I tried to exorcise demons from my life. After they were done, I felt it was time to open up again, and try to recapture that same vision and passion I'd had with my early work.

By this time I was supporting myself through writing full-time (just!) but I was aware that I needed to reach a wider audience if I was to maintain this idyllic state. I needed to combine fantasy with a more mainstream approach. I was told it was called dark fantasy. My contribution to this genre was the Grigori trilogy, which came about through a chain of coincidences.

While I was writing *Calenture* I received a letter from a writer called Andy Collins, who was notorious for having produced the controversial book, *The Black Alchemist*. He told me he had heard I was interested in the subject of the Nephilim and the fallen angels and that he was writing a book about them. To cut a long story short, Andy and I eventually met up and became friends. He and his then partner, Debbie Benstead, would come to stay with me and we'd have blissful weekends of late night drinking and chat about the subjects in which we were passionately interested. Andy was researching the book that would eventually become *From the Ashes of Angels*. One day he asked me why I had never written a novel about the Nephilim. I replied that I thought the subject was too big and couldn't see how it could be done successfully. Andy then said he thought I could do it, especially if I worked from his research notes for his non-fiction book. He wanted *Ashes* to be quite academic, and a lot of the material he'd acquired, through magical and visualisation work, was too off the wall to appear in such a book. But it was perfect for fiction. Thus began a working relationship that is still strong.

The trilogy was bought by Penguin, which, with the benefit of hindsight, I might have avoided, but for all my interest in magic, I'm not that psychic!

All of the magic in the Grigori books is based upon existing practices (past or present), and most of the visionary material is based around the psychic work of Debbie Benstead. The second book *Scenting Hallowed Blood* included experiences that Deb and Andy had had themselves in Cornwall during one of their psychic quests. Azumi, the lion simulacrum in the cliffs, actually exists, complete with eyes, ears and whiskers. You can go to The Lizard and sit on top of his head, but I can't guarantee you'll be able to open up a gateway into the underworld of Albion! (Incidentally, 'Azumi' was the name for the lion guardian that Deb picked up psychically.) All of the sites in the book exist in reality, including the scrying cave of the Pelleth. There is, reputedly, even an order of witches in the area who are known as the Peller. I'd like to say here, though, that the fictional characters in my book are not based upon these people, other than a similarity in name, as I have no idea of their practices and beliefs, although Deb did pick up psychic information at The Lizard, concerning a goddess called Seference.

In creating Peverel Othman – Shemyaza – I felt I had found someone who was equal to Cal and his Wraeththu peers. The fallen angels were dark, mysterious and compelling. While I was writing the books, I felt their presence very near. Also, the material touched me in a very physical way. On more than one occasion, I found myself looking over my shoulder as I was writing, my neck prickling, as if I was being observed, especially in the early hours of the morning. During *Stealing Sacred Fire*, when it came to the time that I had to write the scene prior to Shem's entry into the Crystal Chambers (I won't say more so I don't reveal the plot for anyone who hasn't read it), I felt physically sick. That was the hardest scene I'd ever written.

I am extremely pleased with the way the Grigori trilogy turned out, and know that, technically, they are superior to the Wraeththu books, but they are not the same. *I* am not the same. The experiences I've had since I wrote my first books mean I can never recapture that innocence. I've had to toughen up, become more cynical. To write more Wraeththu books now would be very difficult, because they would inevitably barely resemble the early trilogy. And this might disappoint the readers who are fond of those books. The scene that inspired the trilogy was ephemeral. Goth died, reinvented itself, and exists now in the fringe of alternative culture. It has changed immensely. But Cal, Pellaz and the rest are immortal. They will never fade and die, but continue to exist as I first knew them, untainted by changing fads and fashions. I do not want bitterness or disillusionment to pollute their world.

I am thankful that my American publishers, Tor, have kept the Wraeththu trilogy in print, because they vanished long ago in the UK. I am thankful too for the American readers who are only just coming to my work, mainly through the support of my new publishers, Meisha Merlin and Stark House Press, publications like Carpe Noctem, and long-standing fans like Paul Cashman, who have talked about my work on the web. It's really weird, because I get mail from people who think I am a 'new' writer, whereas for me, the Wraeththu books seem almost antique!

I am lucky in that I can do what I most love to earn a modest living, but it is not an easy way. In order to remain true to myself, and what I believe in, I have had to make sacrifices, but I shall never do anything but write from the heart. There are a thousand new worlds to explore, and I have enough synopses for novels to fill the next ten years. The fact that you, a reader, are looking at this page now, means there are people out there waiting to share those worlds. I hope you enjoy the journey.

This piece was, of course, written before the muse associated with Wraeththu came back into my life, full of ideas and stories. My bitterness at the publishing industry was clear in this piece, which inevitably led to me creating Immanion press in 2003. That was also the year that my revisions of the first Wraeththu trilogy were published, as well as the first volume of the second trilogy, 'The Wraiths of Will and Pleasure'.

On the Subject of Fanfiction

Interview with Mischa Laurent from my old
forum/noticeboard January 2001

Fanfiction seems to be a subject that is cropping up with
increasing regularity, so I thought it was time I made public my
opinion of it. Frequent forum visitor Mischa started the ball
rolling with some interesting questions, and I've reproduced
our initial discussion below.

Mischa:

As a fan of yours and also as a fan of Anne Rice's early books,
I've found the two interests colliding this week and so I seek to
ask you this question. I am wondering what your opinion of
fanfiction is? In the last six months Anne Rice has twice
attacked fan fiction writers with threats of legal action, where
once she used to support fanfiction, even through to linking
from her official page to some of the better fanfic sites.

I read the Anne Rice discussion boards quite often and there
has been much debate on the general status of fanfic on the net
and the attitude of authors and copyright owners to it. Some
people have been asking if anyone knew of any author's
specific opinions on the subject and I immediately thought of
you. So, what would you feel (not do) if you found people
writing fanfiction based on your books? Would you be
flattered? Encouraging? Would you like it or would you rather
your characters remained yours, in the personal, not the legal
sense? No-one who writes fanfic disputes ownership, just the
opposite, so this is an entirely personal question, not one
involving legalities.

Storm:

As long as people give credit where credit is due – i.e. give a
clear explanation concerning from where any characters or

worlds derive, I have no objection to other stories being written about them. I wouldn't be too impressed if people tried to pass it off as their own invention, of course, or if they radically changed the philosophy and themes behind my work. I would also be concerned if there was any confusion over authorship of such stories, in that I wouldn't want the mistake made that any of it derived directly from me. But if a disclaimer about these issues appeared with any piece on the web, I wouldn't have any objection. I might want to take people to task over some of their interpretation, however! But I'd find such discussions really interesting.

I wouldn't like it if I read a story someone had written about the Wraeththu or the Grigori, and they'd taken the themes off in a wildly different direction. It might sound precious, but I'd expect any serious admirer of my work to want to stick to the ambience and beliefs that permeate my books. That doesn't mean I don't think they shouldn't explore those beliefs further – extend the philosophical argument, if you like – but if they want to write something completely different, then they should create their own characters to use as a voice to get their opinions across.

When I first began writing as a child, I created my own kind of fanfiction, in that I wanted to know more about some of the Classical Greek heroes and heroines I read about. I wrote my own sequels to a lot of myths. So I am entirely sympathetic with the drive to explore a fictional world in greater depth.

I think that when an author creates a world and the characters who live in it, then releases it into the public domain, in some ways it grows and develops on its own in the minds of those who read it, and especially those who really get into it. People might fantasise about fictional characters in their heads, and writing those ideas down is just an extension of that. No author has control over such things. It's only when someone tries to publish those ideas that they might come into conflict with the original author.

Similarly, an author has no control over how people

interpret their work. You only have to look at the reviews on Amazon to see the widely differing interpretations of a single book.

Some stories that might have started as fanfiction, such as those written in H P Lovecraft's Cthulhu universe, are now accepted as a legitimate genre, which continues to thrive long after his death. Lovecraft himself encouraged younger and newer writers to explore his ideas, and there are a couple of story collections he had a hand in editing. In this way, I suppose, he retained a certain amount of control over what his fans wrote.

So, that was the initial discussion, and since then I've looked at a web site Mischa recommended. *(Author's Note: site now taken down.)*

I don't have much empathy with Ms Rice's position. I've always looked on my readers as the sole reason I can continue to get my work published. Without them, I wouldn't have a career, so turning on them nastily seems rather counter-productive to me. Perhaps Ms Rice saw a couple of pieces that annoyed her, or that did something with her characters she didn't like, but I would imagine that all fanfic writers would be open to the original authors commenting on their stories, so she could have voiced her complaints without resorting to litigation. These are *fans*, who are *into* her work. I don't believe they intended to upset her, and I'm pretty sure they would have removed or amended offending items. They are not publishing rivals, but simply people into the characters and world of a particular book, or series of books. You can't stop anyone fantasising, so it seem pointless to me getting angry about it. Also, I would imagine that it would be impossible to eradicate the phenomenon completely – you can only drive it further underground.

Still, not being aware of what changed Ms Rice's mind, and not wanting to be unfair to her without knowing all the facts, I tried to imagine a story line of mine that I wouldn't like to see changed. As an example, let's imagine someone wrote a Wraeththu fanfic that changed Wraeththu biology and had them all as ranting Christians or something. How would I react? I'd email the author and point out that if they wanted a different race, with a different belief system, it wouldn't be Wraeththu, so they should think up their own terms for it and disassociate it with my work. If the author became aggressive with me, and didn't want to enter into discussion about it, or flatly refused to put my comments on their site, I'd simply mention it on my site and make clear I do not support their effort and that it does not give a sympathetic rendition of what Wraeththu represents. Given what I know of fanfic writers, having been introduced to quite a few of them now, I'd be surprised if any of them would be that difficult about it.

I suppose, in essence, the arguments for and against are all down to what fanfic really is. Is it a shared world venture, whereby the authors want to write within a world that has already been established, or is it simply an exercise in which writers want to express their own, private fantasies about what they'd do with that world and characters if they were theirs? I don't know enough about it to judge, really. I suspect there are different levels of fanfic, and that both of the above explanations are feasible. I had a good trawl on the web to look at some fanfic and found some very literary examples, written by people who were clearly very much into the worlds concerned, (and who were often very good writers), but there was also a lot of light-hearted porn (especially on the sites devoted to TV series characters). I think it's pretty clear from those sites that the authors do not intend their work to be seen as serious additions to the existing work, but just a saucy excursion into the territory to have a bit of fun.

I did of course eventually go into publishing the best of the Wraeththu fan fiction, which I now see as 'shared world' rather than simply fanfic. Mischa began a full length novel, which I intended to publish, but then vanished from the fan community and I had no further contact. Wraeththu novels are now commissioned and there are regular collections of short stories. See the list of Wraeththu Mythos novels at the end of this book.

Tulpas

Noticeboard Post 14th Jan 2001

There is still quite a lot I want to say about the subject of fan fiction, and in a reply today to an email enquiry about it, I touched upon the subject of tulpas. This also relates to a couple of comments that have appeared on the noticeboard about 'imaginary friends'.

A tulpa is a Tibetan idea and is a term to describe a thought-form externalised into the world so that it has a kind of 'virtual' existence in our reality. I realised that, in some ways, fictional characters are, or become, tulpas, and these are my thoughts on it.

If a mystic or shaman creates a tulpa, generally to carry out some kind of task of a magical nature, it can be perceived with the senses. Other people can see it. A quite famous example is when the renowned Wiccans, Janet and Stuart Farrar, created a thought form they named Mara to protect some seals that were being threatened by hunters. Several people reported seeing a woman in the location where the Farrars had placed the tulpa that fitted the description of how they'd visualised her. (The full description of this is in one of the Farrars' books, but unfortunately I can't remember which one.)

A tulpa is created by feeding a thought or an idea with energy and then putting a mask on that energy, a physical appearance. It's my belief that this is pretty much how gods are created too. The energy of the universe cannot be perceived directly through our primitive senses, and as humans find it difficult to work with formless blobs of energy, we tend to anthropomorphise it, give it faces and personalities, whether that's a patriarchal father god or a nurturing mother goddess. When thousands, if not millions, of human minds all feed the same thought form with their energy, (by believing in it), I think they actually give it a kind of external existence. It is so real, for so many people, that it becomes real. It is concentrated energy, fuelled by intention, will and purpose. This is why we can petition god forms to work on our behalf, whether through prayer, worship or ritual.

Fictional characters are not gods, of course, but they too can be fed with enormous amounts of energy. I've said this a lot of times before, in different interviews and articles, but I'll say it again here because it's relevant: readers are co-conspirators in the creation of a book. It is recreated anew in the mind of each new reader, because that reader will inevitably have a different perspective and visualisation of the world/characters than the writer did and indeed any other reader. Therefore, they feed the idea with their own energy, through their attention to it.

What happens when we read a book? We pick it up, open it, and start to read. From the very first sentence, we begin to create a picture from the word clues given to us by the writer. But they *are* just clues. No writer goes into every tiny specific detail about their worlds, because if they did, the book would be tedious and unreadable and hardly financially viable as it would have to be thousands of pages long. Therefore, the reader does most of the work. Their imagination fills in the blanks and creates the whole picture. I know from reading the postings here that everyone has different views about the Wraeththu characters, and no two people will visualise a single character exactly the same. But the essence of the character, which stems from the writer, remains constant.

When someone is inspired to write their own story about someone else's character, it is not stealing or even being too lazy to create their own, because in one way, they *have* created that character. They have lived with it and its experiences, both pleasant and unpleasant. They identify with it. All writers have to accept that once they have released their work into the public domain, they no longer have quite the same ownership over it that they did when it was just files on their computer. (I'm not talking about mundane copyright issues here, but something less tangible.) Presumably, the writers want people to love their characters, and it's quite understandable that fans might want to know more about a particular world than the writer has time and/or inspiration to provide. Who is any writer to demand that fans should not think about the characters they love, and perhaps even fantasise about them, extend their lives? If I had the time to write the full story of every single character in Wraeththu, then I would, but I don't, and I certainly don't mind if others feel the urge to do so instead.

When a writer puts passion and energy into a book, I think they create a kind of tulpa. It has a life of its own, in that it continues to grow in the minds of its readers. I'm not saying that you can look up from the page and find an image of Pell or Cal standing in the room with you (though I'm sure that few of you would object!), but you are tapping into, and feeding, a pool of energy that other readers before you have invested into the story. It is the same for any well-loved fictional world.

Author Shocked by Complimentary Review

Noticeboard post 16th August 2001

Author Storm Constantine has expressed her thoughts on the review of her latest novel, *The Way of Light* in SFX magazine. 'Frankly, I'm shocked,' she said today. 'This isn't the kind of thing I expect from this magazine. Not only was my work described as 'literary fantasy', but the reviewer also praised my skills at characterisation and dialogue. There wasn't one snide put-down or biased insult. I would have liked to see at least one reference to the fact I can't write. I even came away from reading the review feeling slightly pleased, and that surely isn't normal. SFX is usually immensely unsupportive of my novels and it seems sad that this grand tradition has been overturned by some maverick reviewer, who clearly recognises a good read when he sees one.'

Oh, that felt soooo good!

Wraeththu and Me:
Older, Wiser and Fearless

Web Site Post April 2003

The concept of Wraeththu came to me a long time ago – way back around 1977. After a lifetime of being into the strange and otherworldly, I had just started reading seriously about magic, and the alchemical idea that the human soul is androgynous. I had begun researching angels, with the idea that they were something other than fluffy little chubby things that adorned Christmas and Valentine cards. And I had also been captivated by Mary Renault's novel, *The Persian Boy*. At the same time, I discovered William Burroughs' novel *The Wild Boys*. Wraeththu undoubtedly came from all these influences: ingredients thrown into the cauldron of my imagination, where they were left to simmer and bubble until cooked.

For some years, I toyed with the idea of Wraeththu, without writing any fiction specifically about them. I was engrossed in my first fantasy novel exercise – a plotless meandering extravaganza of purple prose, which one day I might rewrite. *Sign for the Sacred* was set in the same world. Meanwhile, I wrote poems about Wraeththu, and all the time, the idea for that first novel was slowly building in my mind. It wasn't until 1984 that I actually got down to writing it properly.

I remember I was sitting at work, engaged in the thankless task of data input into the library catalogue system. Although I worked with books, which I much appreciated, I certainly did not appreciate the grind of working nine-to-five for local government, with all its petty tyrannical excesses. It might sound harsh, but it seemed to me that several failures as human beings, who with hindsight had no sense of personal power whatsoever, found some kind of identity in the backwater stacks of the county library by ruling their minions with a consuming pettifoggery that beggared belief. I was bored senseless by it all and frustrated beyond description by the small-mindedness I saw around me. One afternoon, I sat at the wretched data input monitor and thought, *Is this to be my life for ever?* It was a sober thought. In a moment of rather furious clarity, I cleared the screen and wrote: 'Today, a perfect day for thinking back.'

This was to become the first line of 'The Enchantments of Flesh and Spirit.'

Almost in a daze, I wrote the first few paragraphs. There were no printers attached to the consoles, so I had to copy what I wrote furtively in longhand, my spine prickling in dread that one of the overseers would notice what I was doing. If that had happened, it's extremely likely that the first paragraphs would have been lost, as I'd have been ordered to clear the screen and get on with my work. Thankfully, a guardian angel must have been standing at my back with a raised sword. I copied down my writing without arousing suspicion. At the end of the day, I went home and disappeared into my bedroom. I wrote copiously.

At the time, I was sharing the house with members of a band – who later became part of the Wraeththu mythos as 'The Closets of Emily Child'. While everyone was socialising downstairs, I began to release the story that had been brewing inside me for years. When I'd finished the first chapter, I went down to the kitchen where a few of my friends were gathered. I felt almost delirious – in another world. But I couldn't share what I was doing. I was intensely private about my work back then. I told my friends I'd been writing, and they said, 'oh, great', and went back to their conversation. I didn't mind. I was on a high. I knew I was going to change my life.

Eventually, as the chapters grew, I realised that if I actually wanted to sell this book, I had to get over my squeamishness about others reading my work. I began with my friends, naturally. The manager for the 'Closets', Dave Weight, was the person who encouraged me to continue. He also helped place the book for me, because he wasn't the least bit scared about pushing and selling an idea. While he did this, I skulked in the background, cringing with shame. It's most peculiar, but I think many writers feel like that to start with.

I've written many times about the good luck that accompanied me trying to find a publisher for *Enchantments*, and won't go into it again, but suffice to say the gods were with me and, with the help of the staff of Andromeda book shop in Birmingham, I sold the book to the first publisher who saw it. I had a lot of work to do on it, as I had yet to learn all the technicalities of writing a novel. While I was rewriting it, I became involved with a Wiccan coven, which opened my eyes further on the subject of magic. This experience was invaluable in helping me to write the story. However, I found rapidly that Wicca was not for me. It didn't scratch the itch for knowledge I had. I wanted something more challenging. This prompted me to start my own magical group with a few friends, which allowed me to be more creative with ritual.

I tried to incorporate some of the ideas I'd come up with for the books, namely that godforms could be androgynous, but I lacked the experience to realise this fully as a functional magical system. It was like writing fiction: I had the wonderful images in my head, but lacked the knowledge and experience to make it real. So, I dropped this idea for many years.

While I was writing that first trilogy, the world of Wraeththu consumed me. I had no idea that the atmospheres, emotions and scents of a fictional world could be so powerful. I knew that I was only scratching the surface, that I was a novice with a lot to learn, but trusted that the universe would let me develop my ideas in relative peace.

Wrong.

I wrote several new Wraeththu synopses after I'd finished the trilogy, but the publishers weren't interested. The books had been plagued by warehouse screw ups, bad distribution, an unfortunate experiment in book size (the then berated 'B format' which often didn't fit on book shop shelves), and lack of publicity and promotion. Even though a lot of critics forgave the glaring errors in style and narrative, and hailed the books as ground-breaking and daring, and I quickly gathered a loyal coterie of fans, the publishing industry saw it differently. Wraeththu, as with countless other creative projects, had been nothing more than a new idea they'd thrown at the wall. It hadn't stuck. It hadn't sold by the bucketload. So, as far as they were concerned, it should be quietly taken outside and drowned. Certainly no new Wraeththu books should be written.

This was such a kick to my gut it left me feeling physically winded. It also inspired the bitter and savage *The Monstrous Regiment*, which is my least favourite of my novels. I was told that if I wanted to continue writing, I'd have to produce something different. Well, MR was certainly that.

I know now that the training I had, by having to jump through all those publishing industry hoops in order to keep a career, was invaluable in helping me grow as a writer. After a couple of years, as I embarked upon the four novels I produced for Headline (*Hermetech*, *Burying the Shadow*, *Sign for the Sacred* and *Calenture*), Wraeththu seemed like an adolescent dream. I suppose I lost my faith in it a bit. I had imagined early success, mainly because the publishers had led me to believe that would happen, but Wraeththu had let me down. Despite constant pleas from readers, asking for more Wraeththu stories, I always said firmly that I doubted I'd go back to that world again. I could see the flaws in the novels now. They were juvenilia. I still had great affection for them, but thought I just had to move on. I'd been told categorically that no one would publish another Wraeththu book.

There is no doubt that I earned the reputation of being 'a writer who doesn't sell'. My work was considered worthy, but perhaps too challenging for the average fantasy reader. It fell between two stools: fantasy on the one hand and literary fiction on the other, alienating readers from both camps, because literary readers scorned fantasy and fantasy readers didn't want anything too highbrow. Many times, I was encouraged to abandon the fantasy format, to write straight fiction – and *Thin Air* was the nearest I came to that. But I found it incredibly hard to do: my heart just wasn't in it. Writing the Magravandias Chronicles after *Thin Air* was such a relief. It made me realise that I must follow my heart.

In the early 90s, I visited the American convention, Dragon*Con, for three years running, and was lucky enough to be introduced on my first visit to Stephe Pagel, who had just set up his own publishing company, Meisha Merlin. Stephe was interested in my work and wanted to bring out a US edition of my Grigori trilogy. I have no doubt whatsoever that Stephe's support, which raised my profile in the US, was a great influence, (if only in the ethers!), on the Magravandias Chronicles being bought by TOR. They had not purchased anything from me since the Wraeththu days, even though the omnibus edition of the trilogy was still in print and selling well. Meisha Merlin, and then Stark House, began bringing out my back catalogue. Some of the books had been out of print for years, and I was delighted and grateful that these companies were behind me.

Once I'd finished writing the Magravandias Chronicles, I had to come up with a new idea. Then it struck me. I knew it was time to go back to the world of Wraeththu. I knew what happened next.

The other synopses I'd written, just after *Fulfilments of Fate and Desire* came out, did not involve any of the characters from the original books. I realised that in order to go back to that world, I wanted to take up the story where it left off. I was older, as the characters were older. For the first time in years, I felt a familiar heady excitement. That world hadn't left me. I might have lost faith in it, but it seemed as if it had continued regardless without me. And it did not bear a grudge. It welcomed me back.

I spoke to my UK editor about the idea and she also thought it was a good one. Unfortunately, people higher in the company were rather less enthusiastic. I was made to wait for nearly a year before my editor said 'no'. Meanwhile, the synopsis had gone to TOR in the States, and Beth Meachem, my editor there, got back to me within a week saying, 'yes please!'

I was unprepared for the massive support that came from the Wraeththu fan base. It was as if Wraeththu was given a new lease of life all over the world. Web sites devoted to it and its fan fiction sprang up, most especially Mischa Laurent's 'Forever' site and Trish's 'Wraeththu Companion', an online encyclopaedia. Wendy Darling revived 'Inception' (originally a magazine and info service), creating a dynamic and colourful new web site. Wendy also launched 'Procreation', another Wraeththu fanfic site. The Wraeththu egroup on Yahoo (set up some years ago by Opium Poppy Fields, another long-time supporter), became more active and attracted new members.

Pillowed by all this encouragement, I began to write, and it was as if I'd opened a vein: the story poured out.

There are some plot spoilers about to occur now. So skip the next sections if you haven't already read *Wraiths of Will and Pleasure* and are intending to do so.

The new material, while sharing the atmosphere and otherworldliness of the original books, is certainly different. I think that some Wraeththu fans might find it difficult to start with, but I hope they'll stick with it, reread it, and get into what I am now trying to do. It is grittier, more realistic and far less idealistic. In the first books, I sort of dithered round some aspects of androgyny, not least the case of reproduction. In *Wraiths*, this is confronted full on. I have to thank my good friend, Paula Wakefield, for her assistance in writing the pearl birthing scene that takes place in the Kakkahaar camp near the beginning of the book. Paula read my first draft, pursed her lips in the way only she can, and then started making suggestions. She showed me how to make it real and frightening, how it might actually *be* for creatures who had once been human males to deal with it. Not having had children myself, nor ever having had the desire to do so, my knowledge in this area was lacking, but my creative side was delighted with what Paula told me about it. I wanted to create a rank visceral event, because this would be so much more shocking to the hara involved, seeing as a blissful, spiritually elevated form of aruna had occasioned it.

The original books had explored the Wraeththu in terms of romantic emotion, now I wanted to get under their skins. Many readers had asked me to expand upon the Kamagrian, and this indeed occurs in *Wraiths*. The whole concept of gender pronouns had rattled critics, back in the early days, who had simply seen hara as gay men, because I used a masculine pronoun for them. It occurred to me as I was writing *Wraiths* that hara would have used this term, because it was what they had always used to refer to themselves. So how would that affect Kamagrian, those rare females who were incepted to Wraeththu? My characters pretty much told me, as the writing continued to pour, that they felt uncomfortable referring to themselves as 'he': they also wanted to use the term with which they were familiar and felt comfortable. This was an interesting concept to explore.

In the original books, I wrote that Kamagrian were always born to Wraeththu hara, as freak births, but unexpectedly, as I was writing the new book, Pell's sister Mima became incepted accidentally, through the spilled blood of Lileem, a Kamagrian harling. How she deals with this, and also how she cannot help but view Lileem as female, inform a greater part of the story. I realised that much of the former humans' identity derived from their early life experiences, no matter what had happened to them since. Mima could not simply wake up one day and start thinking of herself as 'he'. But at the same time, she wanted to be accepted as a normal har. The Kamagrian really do have a rough deal, and this is mainly down to the politics of their leader, Opalexian, who is opposed to the idea of parazha and hara ever coming together. Admittedly, the conjunction of Wraeththu and Kamagrian energies does have some devastating effects, but even as I was writing Opalexian, I could not agree totally with her views. There are ways in which both species could experiment safely with one another, but this is not allowed. Aruna between parazha and hara opens portals to other worlds, which is dangerous, but this could be controlled. Simply being aware of the risks could prevent disaster, but unfortunately the character of Opalexian is too strong, and she wouldn't let me explore that area in the story. Well, not yet.

I could write a whole article about how characters tend to develop a life of their own as you work with them: an experience I know many other writers, especially fantasy writers, share. At the time of writing, I am into the last quarter of the second new Wraeththu novel *The Shades of Time and Memory*. I know, as I once more take pleasure in the act of writing, that I was right to follow my heart. I am not the person I was all those years ago, grateful for simply being published and willing to be blown about by the random winds of the industry. I have come to take charge of my life, to do what matters. The Wraeththu and I thank all of you.

New Steps from Saltrock
Wraeththu Revisited
Preface to the 2003 revised edition of 'The Enchantments of Flesh and Spirit'

For quite a few years, I'd fended off readers' pleas for more Wraeththu material. My argument was that I wrote the original books fifteen years ago, and I had changed too much as a writer ever to revisit that territory and do it justice. A certain innocence and naivety has disappeared from my work, and that naïve voice was part of what made the Wraeththu books special work. Some readers agreed with me and felt the Wraeththu should be left alone in their world of the past.

However, recently I changed my mind. I don't know what the catalyst was exactly, but it was as if I received a communication from a friend with whom I'd lost touch. Suddenly, I knew what happened next, after the end of the trilogy.

It occurred to me that if I were trying to sell a new Wraeththu book, it wouldn't do any harm to try and persuade a publisher to reissue the original trilogy. The books are still in print in the US, but I thought it would be good for them to reappear in the UK, especially as they were marketed so dismally the first time round.

Out came the reading copy of the Wraeththu trilogy from my book shelf, dusty and yellowed with age. I didn't have a copy of any of the books on my computer, as I'd written the first two on a manual typewriter and the third on an Amstrad word processor, which I gave away a long time ago. Stupidly, I didn't think to translate the files before I did so – I have a drawer full of those chunky old disks. The thought of typing the books up again was not a pleasant one. I have little enough spare time as it is and I envisioned it would take me forever to do the job. I realised I'd have to scan the books into my computer.

The software I'd previously used for such operations wasn't brilliant and it had been quicker to type material manually, but luck was on my side, because I'd recently acquired a new scanner, and the software it came with made scanning and OCR (changing a graphic into text) a doddle.

One thing quickly became obvious as I put the pages into a master document. *The Enchantments of Flesh and Spirit* was very evidently a first novel, littered with plot holes, bad grammar and sections that were, frankly, badly written. The opening chapter in particular was a mess. As I read it, wincing, it seemed to me that I found my feet round about the place in the story where Pellaz first becomes Wraeththu. The novel flowed more smoothly thereafter. More than anything, as I scrolled through the pages, I wanted to re-edit the book, and also add more material to fill in the gaping holes. *Bewitchments of Love and Hate* and *Fulfilments of Fate and Desire* were more accomplished, and would need less editing, but the first one – ouch!

Also, because I was writing a new trilogy, with a wealth of writing experience behind me, certain aspects of the original books would be inconsistent with better ideas I'd had since. These inconsistencies needed to be ironed out.

For those of you who have not read this book before, I advise skipping the next few paragraphs, because they contain plot spoilers.

I talked to a friend about the book and she had a lot of useful things to say. She must be one of the biggest fans of the Wraeththu books, and she was concerned that in grooming the text of *Enchantments*, some of its magic might be lost. She agreed that the writing wasn't brilliant and that there were a lot of holes in the plot, but for the same reason that many people still love Andy Collins' first book, *The Black Alchemist*, (which

I'm sure Andy would be the first to agree suffered from similar inexperience with writing), the shaky writing skill doesn't get in the way of the story and in some regard actually makes it work. As *Enchantments* was written from a first person viewpoint, the voice was ostensibly Pell's, not mine. To a reader, if he didn't give all the information about his world, it was because he didn't possess it.

While I could appreciate this, I pointed out that to me Pell's naïve voice was misplaced, because in the book, by the time he came to write his story, he wasn't an ignorant sixteen year old, but ruler of the Wraeththu. The way it was written, it was more like a diary, with the initial chapters being told in that immature manner. But it isn't a diary, it's an historical narrative and Pell's voice should remain consistent throughout, otherwise it does not make much sense. My friend agreed – rather grudgingly! – but still insisted that the melancholy mood of the story might be lost if I tinkered with it too much.

Well, that was the responsibility I was taking on – improving the book without damaging it. I hoped that with the experience I'd gained, I would be able to do this.

The first thing I wanted to address was the background to the world at the beginning of the story. It was patently obvious that when I first wrote the book, I really wasn't interested in background, but just wanted to tell the tale of the characters. As a more experienced writer, this made me extremely uncomfortable. As I reread it, I thought it really wouldn't take much to make the world more convincing. The strange weather and landscape in Pell's homeland – a mix of different climates, it seems – could be explained somewhat by global climate changes. I also thought that the travellers who pass through Pell's village bearing tales of Wraeththu from the north could give more information about the breakdown of society. As it stood, it was very sketchy and far too convenient. Wraeththu had risen from the ghettoes of inner cities, from the ranks of disaffected youths. In many ways they had changed and had left their humanity behind, but in others they had not: they had reverted to a more barbaric kind of humanity. The only way they could have spread so quickly and relatively easily was if the world was already experiencing terrible problems, whether they were natural catastrophes, plague, world war, or civil strife. (For example, if certain volcanoes in the Mediterranean area should erupt ferociously, the eastern seaboard of the US could be utterly taken out by tidal waves for up to twenty miles inland.)

I wanted to rectify the flimsiness and make the world come alive for the reader, to place Pell and his fellow characters in context. I didn't intend to pile on a lot of tedious exposition, but give clearer yet lightly sketched information.

Having now completed this rewrite, I have found that it's grown far more than I thought it would. And it hasn't just been background material. I found that the characters had more opinions about their condition and questions about their world.

As a character, Pellaz was, quite simply, problematic, at least in the initial chapters of the book. He described himself as a peasant, but as his father is overseer of the farm, his family are hardly a bunch of serfs. They have the biggest house in the village. I also think now that no one would refer to themselves as a 'peasant'. It is a derogatory term, usually used as an insult. Pell implied his life was hard, and said that his country was cruel, petty and bitter, which was reflected in the people. Again, there was no evidence for this. Quite the contrary. Pell's life, as a favoured son, far from the turmoil and terror of the northern cities, seemed idyllic.

Pellaz left his home with Cal far too readily, which given what he'd heard about the Wraeththu seemed downright stupid. Cal had bewitched him, of course, but Pell hardly questioned his strong, overwhelming reaction to an utter stranger. Given that he's quite intelligent, I didn't give him enough of a reason simply to walk out of the life he knows. I said he was escaping hardship, but there wasn't much hardship to escape. He was loved, admired and favoured by his family, his sister Mima especially. It was all down to Cal and I really thought this needed to be emphasised a little more.

Pell is educated, which was explained away somewhat glibly by his having been given lessons by the local priest. This, incidentally, was not mentioned until too late in the story, when it obviously occurred to me that Pell's voice was not that of an illiterate. The information needed to be moved nearer to the beginning of the novel and fleshed out slightly.

Pell also berated himself all the time about how terrible and selfish his behaviour was, which really it wasn't. If he reacted badly to something, it was usually with just cause. He continually made negative assumptions about how Cal perceived him, yet implied that his family spoilt him, which didn't sit well with all the carping self-deprecation. Spoilt children generally think quite highly of themselves.

Pell didn't ask enough questions about where and what he was going to, and was too easily placated by people like Flick and Seel, who really didn't give him the information he needed. Also, the fact that people believe all Wraeththu to be exclusively homosexual was hardly explored. Surely, for any potential convert, this would be an important factor to consider. Pell answered Cal's somewhat ham-fisted queries about his sexuality with haste and dismissal. But privately, if not openly, he would surely think more about it. He would question his own motives for leaving home so readily with Cal to join a bunch of aggressive outcasts, for whom – it appears – being gay was mandatory. Right from the beginning, he *has* to think about how he'll have to sleep with what he thinks are men – or at least Cal – and he *must* have an opinion about it. It's feasible he could push the thoughts away and decide to deal with them later when the bridge looms up to be crossed, but for the sake of realism, this should be shown in the story. His prime motive for leaving home is not that he yearns to be Wraeththu, but because he's fascinated by Cal and wants to be with him. The Wraeththuness, initially, is incidental. It's only later, once they reach Saltrock, that Pell realises exactly what he's got into. He's young and naïve, but in the original version seemed utterly stupid and ignorant, as if he didn't think about anything. (People *can* be like that, but if that were the case the older Pell writing the story would have had something to say about it.)

When he finally decided he was disappointed Cal hadn't initiated anything physical between them, the idea seemed to pop out of nowhere. I felt this had to be dealt with, because it should have been the driving force of the beginning of the novel.

I saw that the problems could be fixed easily with just minor adjustments to the text and perhaps a little more inner dialogue on Pell's part. I also thought that there should be more conversation between Cal and Pell on their journey to Saltrock, so that Pell could ask some questions about his future. It didn't mean Cal had to answer them – truthfully – but at least it would be more realistic.

Some aspects of the story, particularly the night before Pell is incepted, are horrific. The moment when he realises what is going to happen to him and that he cannot escape it is chilling. Well, the idea was, but I don't think the actual writing really conveyed it. Wraeththu has aspects of a sinister cult: once someone knows the truth, they cannot be allowed to leave unchanged. Pell knows hardly anything and walks blindly right into it. There wasn't enough realism to his reactions and inner thoughts. There was no good reason given as to why he wanted to be Wraeththu. If the answer was because of Cal, then it needed to be shown more. Pell was too accepting of everything that happened to him in Saltrock, until the moment when he was left alone in the dark with the truth. Yet before that, he'd already known he could die from inception. Despite that knowledge, it didn't occur to him that he was actually a prisoner of Wraeththu and that what was going to be done to him was against his will. Cal had brought him to Saltrock for a reason and Pell didn't even question why. I thought that when he found out what inception was, he'd have been far more angry and frightened. He would have realised how trapped he was, how trusting he'd been of complete strangers and what a stupid thing to do that had been. He'd thought he was joining a hip yet cosy gang. In reality, he was going to be mutated, turned into a creature that was both male and female, and his humanity would be torn from him. Would anyone accept this terrifying change so casually? He did have a bit of an iffy fit in the original, but he got over it far too quickly. He was effectively betrayed by people he trusted, and that is a real turning point in anyone's life. He'd never been betrayed like that before.

I'd already mentioned he had a fear of disfigurement, (when Flick told him he'd lose some of his hair), so having his sexual organs altered would have to have been more horrifying than it was presented in the original version.

I had a lot of gripes with the way Pell was written, but it was mainly in the first couple of chapters. I could see how to fix it, without ruining the mood of the book.

The other character I wanted to do more with was Orien. When I began *Enchantments*, I didn't know that he would die at Cal's hand later on in the novel and in the subsequent drafts didn't bother putting in any narrative clues about this. Now, I thought Orien should have some presentiment of what would happen. I decided that some tension could be shown between him and Cal, which Pell would find perplexing. He believes Orien to be a serene mystic, and can't understand Cal's hostility, but I think Cal always suspected there was more to Orien than meets the eye, which is part of his motive for the subsequent murder. Orien is a complex character, more of a trickster than Cal in many ways. He knows exactly what and who Thiede is, for example, and what Thiede's plans for Pellaz are. He comes across as a wise, gentle healer, but in fact he's capable of being quite hard and callous. I filled out Orien's character in the story 'Paragenesis', which is Thiede's tale of the beginning of

Wraeththu. Orien was the first person to become Wraeththu after Thiede. ('Paragenesis' appeared in the *The Crow: Shattered Lives and Broken Dreams* anthology, edited by James O'Barr). I realised that, in *Enchantments*, Orien must send for Thiede when someone at Saltrock – probably Seel – realises that Pell is special and different to the usual recruits. Cal will tell Seel he is confused about how compelled he was to bring Pell into the Wraeththu fold. What is so different about this boy? It's not just his appearance. Seel would know Cal isn't affected by people that easily, and would discuss it with Orien. Orien knows Thiede is on the lookout for someone 'special' and would therefore send him word that he should perhaps consider visiting Saltrock for an impending inception. As to why Thiede is really looking for that special someone, I suddenly knew the answer, and it's not just that he's looking for a pretty figurehead for the Gelaming. I didn't see Seel as being a conspirator in Thiede's plans, so his surprise at discovering Thiede at the Harhune is genuine, but Orien certainly is a conspirator. A lot went on behind the scenes that Pell didn't know about.

I wrote a new scene where Cal confronts Orien about his suspicions, which as Pell is a spectator meant I could set it in Saltrock. A host of ideas came spilling through about the different factions of Wraeththu and I realised that despite what reviews at the time decreed, there is actually a plot lurking in the story. It just wasn't brought out. Cal accuses Orien of espousing a kind of selective inception program and that Wraeththu from the conflict-torn cities are regarded as a lesser species by tribes such as the Gelaming. He has vowed to find Immanion, but there is a reason for this. It's not just that he wants a nice place to live. Cal is educated, and he feels that the Gelaming should know the truth about what happens in the dark corners of Wraeththu, and that those hara should not just be written off as failed inceptions. He points out that many hara were incepted into the more vicious tribes without knowledge of the alternatives, so how can they be held to blame? From this discussion, a real, whole picture emerged that set Wraeththu in a firm, credible context, answering all those awkward questions like, 'well, if they're so perfect, why do they…' etc.

Wraeththu believe themselves to be the inheritors of the earth and superior to humanity, but the fact is they're just different, the majority of them plagued by the same herd culture and lack of awareness as humans are. They have greater potential, but it's as if their creator has unleashed them on the world to learn by their mistakes – or not. They are mostly misguided and ignorant. They are foragers, living in and off ruins, and very few of them have the cohesion to create a proper society. Their environment means little to them. I also thought their belief system needed some work, because it had no proper structure. There was the odd mention of them working magically with angels, but no explanation as to why they made that choice. Most of the work on this belief system takes place in the new trilogy, beginning with *The Wraiths of Will and Pleasure* (TOR, 2003).

I know that some readers, who are fond of the original books, won't approve of what I've done, but I felt strongly that *Enchantments* could be improved so much it really shouldn't be republished unless the work was done. If anyone's going to be precious about a book, it should surely be the author rather than the readers – and one thing I'm not is precious. *Enchantments* is often enchanting, and in many ways I'm still very proud of my achievement, but it seemed a shame that the story was marred by my initial lack of writing experience. Surely, having been given the opportunity, I should do all that I can to rectify the errors, so that a new generation of readers are given a more rounded and accomplished novel. I remained sensitive to its tone and style and respected all those aspects that have inspired people to love the books. Also, the original books exist and all the rewriting in the world cannot remove them from people's book shelves. Some movie fans love the original version of certain films, while others prefer the director's cut. You have the choice of which one you watch, and it's the same with books.

Fate has guided me towards republishing this book myself, as part of the newly created Immanion Press. I also intend to republish the second and third volumes of the original series in the United Kingdom. As I was doing the work on *Enchantments*, I could imagine Pellaz standing behind me, arms folded, keeping a stern eye on what I was doing. With such an overseer, I must surely have done it the right way!

Wraeththu Inspirations

From *Paragenesis*, Immanion Press, 2010

I've written often about how the Goth scene of the 80s greatly influenced the development of Wraeththu, and this is true insofar as the novels drew upon that scene, but seeing as the concept has been with me since my early teens, its initial influences go much farther back.

I've recently been pondering what first spark set it all off and have been reinvestigating things I was into as a teenager and before – what I can remember. Music has always played a big part in my life and I often think how lucky I was to be young through the tail end of Hippydom, on to the Glam scene of the 70s, later Punk, New Romantics and then Goth. In comparison to what's around nowadays, which seems a bit dreary to me; that was a heady ride! But despite how those flamboyant scenes inspired and directed me, there was one perhaps more crucial influence that I have recently remembered. (Some delving into the hard drive of the mind was required!)

I don't know exactly how young I was, but it was between 7 and 10 years old. Every weekend, my parents used to farm me

out to grandparents so they could indulge in a hedonistic lifestyle, a propensity for which I inherited from them! My father's parents lived in a detached house with a big garden, and after my uncle left home, (he was a lot younger than my Dad), I used to sleep in his old bedroom, which was larger than the one I'd been allocated since a baby. I remember one summer day sitting on the floor in that room, poring through my uncle's book shelves, which contained all the books he'd been given as a child. It was a sunny day, and that quiet time in the afternoon, when all you used to be able to hear was the sounds of kids playing in the distance and bird song. I pulled out a copy of *The Second Jungle Book* by Rudyard Kipling and began to leaf through it. It wasn't an illustrated volume as such, but had large chapter headings, which were like wood cuts. In a couple of these illustrations, the jungle boy Mowgli was depicted, but this was a far cry from how he was portrayed in the later Disney movie. He was shown

as androgynously naked, with streaming hair. I just stared at these images in absolute fascination. They excited me, which I suppose was in some pre-sexual kind of sense, but as well as making me want to read the book, it inspired me to make up my own stories about this gorgeous being. So began my fantasies of the long-haired androgyne. I really think this must have been a defining moment in the creation of Wraeththu. All pictures here are by J Lockwood Kipling, from the original edition of *The Second Jungle Book*.

Thus, with my interest in the androgynous dramatically established, when the Glam Rock scene exploded in a maelstrom of glitter and feather boas in the 70s I was naturally drawn to it. But my introduction to it as an ingenuous school girl was another image that brought me up short. It was either in the girl's magazine *Jackie* (how many UK 40-50 somethings remember *Jackie*?), or *Fab 208*, another required periodical of the fashionable teen. *Fab 208* was connected with Radio Luxembourg, the then cool pirate station to listen to at night. Anyway, back to that image. It was of the band, T Rex, one of their first promotional pictures following the success of their first and second singles in the charts. When I first saw it, I remember actually being surprised, because it so echoed the kind of fantasies I had. For a moment, I experienced a kind of territorial annoyance that other people were tapping into my private dreams. Marc Bolan and Mickey Finn were shown as white-faced and long-haired, with a wistful expression in their eyes that spoke of mystical secrets. These were the creatures of my fantasies made flesh. I didn't have a name for them then;

they just existed as shadowy entities in my head. But somehow, here they were, externalised and in print, and soon to be drooled and swooned over by a battalion of pubescent females. I can remember vividly the disgust I felt at seeing T Rex gig footage on TV, where thousands of sweaty, hysterical teenage girls were screaming at their idols. I was too repulsed even to consider being part of that. Even at that young age, I felt my interest was more aesthetic. I shunned the reaction of the masses, downright infuriated they misunderstood and belittled the allure of these on stage personae.

It can hardly be contested that T Rex were the first 'slashable' band, ('slash' fiction being stories that involve pop culture male figures in homoerotic relationships). Right from the start there were rumours about their sexuality and the whispered suggestion that Bolan and Finn might actually enjoy rather more than a musical relationship. How true these rumours were I have no idea, because it's feasible an outrageously bi-sexual slant  might have been deliberately introduced to increase sales and provoke publicity. You only have to re-watch the movie *Velvet Goldmine* (an accurate portrayal of those times, I think), to see how everyone in the alternative scene of the day suddenly thought it was fashionable to be bi. But I knew nothing of any of that, because I was young, naïve, still at school and my social life revolved around friends who had ponies. (Yes, it's true, even though it changed rather swiftly after that.) I began to write stories inspired by the fantastical public image of T Rex. Bolan and Finn, as the band, were as fictional no doubt as the things I wrote, but I didn't care about that. What is most annoying is that I destroyed a lot of what I wrote, because I went through a phase of being terrified of my parents reading my writing. Even then, I wrote mild 'slash', and I often felt guilty about it. Why, I don't know, because now I don't think my parents would have minded one bit, if in fact they'd ever bothered to read my exercise books full of stories, but schoolgirls can have rather strange ideas about the older generation. What I feared most was that they would laugh. My stories were set in a fantasy world and I really regret now that they didn't survive. I still have a few of them, but so many were lost. In fact, these early stories were set in the world that eventually turned up in Sign for the Sacred, so it's as 'old' as Wraeththu, which is quite bizarre to realise. I began a novel called *Sun Incarnate*, which I still have, even though it never got finished. Mickey Finn was the physical inspiration for the character Micythus, who was the original prototype for Resenence Jeopardy. However, when I finally got round to writing *Sign for the Sacred*, decades later, it was not with all those early influences in mind.

Of course, I can't leave David Bowie out of the equation either. In particular, his album 'Diamond Dogs' was a soundtrack for me to write to, and I think that album was also somewhat inspired by William Burroughs' work. Bowie came prominently onto the scene after T Rex and was another seminal artist of the Glam movement. It's hardly a secret that the film 'Velvet Goldmine' fictionalised (and perhaps fantasised) his relationship with wild child of rock, Iggy Pop. Bowie's on stage antics with his guitarist, Mick Ronson, made headlines and naturally he became another of my muses.

Looking at these two pictures below, of Bowie and Ronson, I think they demonstrate how I visualised the proto-versions of Thiede and Ashmael, even though those characters were created a decade or so after this particular era of music. I see in Bowie's (then) on-stage personae the roots of Thiede: the trickster, the magician, the manipulator, a creature of many colours.

But long before Wraeththu came into being, I began a sequel to *Sun Incarnate*, called *Child of the Morning*, even though I'd never finished the first one. I just had a different story to tell, influenced by new inspirations, although set in the same world. Micythus was still in it, although this time as a secondary character to the main protagonist, Phrynis. *Child of the Morning* was greatly influenced by such writers as Mary Renault and Jane Gaskell. It was the story of a beautiful boy taken into captivity and having to cope with life in a royal harem, beset by bitchery and betrayal. By this time, I'd read *The Persian Boy* by Mary Renault, (but for the fact 'Child' had completely different characters, it was a kind of homage to *The Persian Boy*), and my interests in beautiful, androgynous creatures had truly coalesced. Also, my musical and aesthetical inspirations had moved on. I'd left school and had gone to the local art college.

Round about this time, The New York Dolls – the epitome of proto Punk/Glam sleaze – released their first album. The minute I saw photographs of them in the music press, I knew they were my kind of band. And when I bought the album, I

wasn't disappointed.

'Personality Crisis' and 'Jet Boy' are still classics, and I don't think anyone can deny that The Dolls were a huge influence on alternative music, especially early Punk. They were like something out of a science fiction movie. They belonged in a post holocaust world of sexbots and ravaged cities. There were reports in the music press of guys making out at the back of venues at their shows. The Dolls were another influence on my writing and their weird, almost comic book decadence went into the pot to help create Wraeththu. Round about this time I also discovered William Burroughs' novel, *The Wild Boys* (later to be immortalised by Duran Duran, though in rather censored form!). Blatantly homo-erotic, bizarrely magical, this book I think gave me the courage to write more honestly, and more confidently. Its narrative is hardly linear, and neither can you really engage with any of the characters, but the ideas, and some of the imagery, (especially the tribal stuff), totally captivated me.

Shortly after discovering The Dolls, it was time for The Ramones to make an appearance, and although this band were hardly beings of ambivalent sexuality and glam, the music was great. If anything, it was an extension of the Dolls' dementia. 'I Don't Wanna Go Down to the Basement' and 'Beat on the Brat', were two especial favourites of mine. I also developed a huge crush on Joey Ramone (sadly

now dead), and he made it as physical inspiration into several of my stories in various guises.

It was during these years, from the last year of school and the short time I spent at art college that I wrote the first Wraeththu stories and poems, but I didn't actually come up with the term 'Wraeththu' until a couple of years after that. This was when I had a dreary receptionist's job at a building company, situated out in the middle of nowhere, far from the edge of town on an early industrial estate. We didn't get many visitors. I used to spend my time, when my work for the day was done, writing stories and poems, drawing pictures and reading ancient dictionaries, full of antiquated words. I remember I used to draw pictures of my co-workers as cartoon animals, which for some reason were very popular, even if they weren't always very flattering! When the company finally went into liquidation, I wrote a fantasy tale about the whole sad demise – really should try and dig that out, it had its amusing moments – and gave it to all my colleagues as a keepsake. But during that time, I found the word Wraeththu in an etymological dictionary and for some odd reason fell in love with it. It meant 'wrath' but also 'rake' as in the gardening or farming implement. However, it wasn't the meaning of the word that snared me, just its shape and sound.

For a long while, I left the world of Wraeththu behind, as 'real life' concerns of a more demanding full time job, and a partner who actually resented me writing, came to the fore. But the siren call of that world was not to be denied.

In the very early 80s I discovered my independence, ditched the controlling boyfriend and bought a house, several rooms of which I rented out to friends, including members of the band 'The Closets of Emily Child' whose guitarist became my new partner. This band had a cameo part in *The Enchantments of Flesh and Spirit*, although none of the real people involved actually inspired any of the characters. They just wanted the band to be in the book! These were the days of early Goth, when New Romanticism metabolised into something darker yet in many ways more camp. I began writing my Wraeththu stories again, determined now to finish a novel, egged on and encouraged by the manager of the The Closets, who was there to be Mr Pushy for me when I was too shy and embarrassed to let people see my work. And happily, there was a new generation of musician pretty boys to inspire me.

Bands like Gene Loves Jezebel, Getting the Fear/Into a Circle and Christian Death all had members who physically inspired the characters of Enchantments and its sequels. Jay and Mike Astin from Gene Loves Jezebel certainly helped shape the characters of Cobweb and Terzian respectively. And looking at this old picture of them, it's easy to see why.

Pellaz's earliest inspiration was undoubtedly Johnny Thunders from the New York Dolls (only in his early appearance not in his rather erm... *hedonistic* character), but strangely, I never had a real life person who inspired the look of Cal. He was – and remains – an archetype, almost impossible to capture in a picture.

The idea and shape of Vaysh came from Getting the Fear's vocalist, Bee (below). Later that band became Into a Circle. If you can find any pictures online of the later band's EP covers, you will see why they were an influence for Wraeththu material.

Seel's was inspired physically by Christian Death's David Glass, (below), who in his youth was positively unearthly in appearance.

It's interesting for me to wander back down the memories and recall exactly how the ideas for my fictional characters came together. The living people whose public personae inspired many of the Wraeththu are now twenty or thirty years older, and the enigmatic beauty they once possessed has no doubt long gone. Most of the wild boys of those days have probably now settled down to a humdrum life with wives and children, have become drug burnouts, or are – at worst – dead (quite a few are, come to think of it). I hope that the survivors continue to be creative and successful in their own way. But whatever those shining boys might be doing now, or not, they are immortalised as they were within the pages of the Wraeththu novels.

Jungle Boy Mowgli and Joey Ramone? Unlikely companions perhaps, but they are both part of my formula.

On the Craft of Writing

The Feast of Fiction
Art for the 21st Century
October 1998

As with many articles and essays I've written and have published over the years, where this piece was published and exactly when has been forgotten. I've a feeling it was for a British Fantasy Society publication – but other than that the information has left my memory! I found it intriguing to reread this piece, written as it was at the beginning of the new technological age. Ironically, (given what I say in this piece) the rise of the internet and the creation of eBooks has given fiction a new lease of life. And small publishers have, to a degree, created our Punk revolution in literature, in terms of provocative and non-mainstream novels and stories getting into print. How things have changed in seventeen years.

The knowledge and expertise of the human race advances. Unfortunately, the brains that were agile enough to generate the wildest, unimagined excesses of new technology are perhaps not quite as competent as the micro-chipped beast-children they have engendered. We have not planned for this new future we are designing. As the population burgeons, greedily obliterating the empty spaces upon this, our groaning, green jewel of a world, there are fewer tasks that require the services of a human employee. Factories and power plants are now often quite capable of running themselves, hardly needing wetware – a little person of flesh and blood – to push buttons or pull levers. We are at the brink of acquiring a glorious amount of leisure time, when we should be freed from mundane tasks to pursue our own interests, but an ever-growing proportion of the population is being plunged into penury. Neither does it appear, from this point in time, that the situation will improve. Bewitched by the siren allure of commercials, the new impoverished are led gasping to an oasis that is ever retreating before their outstretched hands, an oasis seething with consumer goods, expensive, fashionable clothes, drinks, foodstuffs, you name it. At the same time, our population is 'greying'; by the year 2000, there will be more 'elderly' people alive on this planet than have ever been alive before. We have new medical technology to extend our lives – unfortunately most of us will be too poor to take advantage of it. People worry more than ever about ageing, with the knowledge that their lives might well be longer but the quality of the twilight years might be extremely poor, depending on how much money/insurance the individual has amassed throughout their life. This has given rise to rampant ageism; fear turned to hate, despising. If you are not young, you are worthless.

The world speeds up.

As longevity expands, life accelerates. What was once a languid stroll from cradle to grave is now a hectic gallop, with the enervated contestant frantically trying to gather up the golden fruits that litter the path. Speed. Flight. Science fiction has become science fact. The frontier of space has already been breached, shattering our dreams. Mars, far from being a red planet of advanced alien culture, perhaps the home of our distant ancestors (as many 50's SF novels would have had us believe), has been revealed as an empty desert. Venus, no longer a veiled jungle planet of mysterious beauty, has been stripped of her secrets and exposed as a poisonous hothouse maelstrom. All the fantasies of Venusians and Martians are bled of life. Now, SF writers are looking for new frontiers to breach, new mysteries of science to explore. They are looking inwards; the last alien frontier is that of the human psyche, the human being in crisis.

We are at a crucial point in our evolution; a make or break time. As the advocates of New Age sing platitudes about the dawning of enlightenment, a millennium of mind expansion and self-development, others, more cynical and desperate, see the event horizon of the end of the world. The new magicians, the quantum physicists, are telling us that both these realities already exist. According to some of the pop physicists, everything you can ever imagine already exists, because space and time are invented things, and there is an infinity of realities just beyond our perceptions. As we are unable to verify this information for ourselves, the 'knowledge' itself becomes meaningless, belief in it an act of faith. (Twenty-first century definition of scientist: priest). So, as science becomes mystified, if not mystifying, its magi divorced from reality in their search for the beatific Theory of Everything, the ordinary world continues to produce the results of the Experiment of Humanity. There seems to be too much of everything: disaster, pollution, monetary collapse, war, people. Everything has gone crazy, like bacteria in a nutrient-rich petri dish. And the lowest common denominator has dominion over all. It has been said that reality itself is but a social construct. Have we then unwittingly created this Pandemonium we now inhabit?

In times of crisis, the function of artists – novelists, musicians, film-makers – has often been to articulate the underlying feelings, the silent cries, of the population. Since the days of cave paintings and myths created in the light of smoke and flame, the created image and the written word have illustrated the essential truths behind and within human experience. But, as the recession bites deep, like an untreated abscess in our society, purse strings snap shut, and the media panic. Any literature, film or music that challenges the reader/observer, that requires a certain amount of effort or participation from the consumer, is seen by the 'money men' who administer the industries as worthless, because it is not hugely commercial. In this environment, the only thing worth investing in is the cheese-burger and fries of literature, music and film. Devoured in minutes, digested without thought, expelled, leaving no trace, except perhaps for some subtle, pernicious cancers. We are gorging on grunge while the world burns. Who has the money, or time, to sit down to the feast? And good fiction is a feast, a banquet of the senses. The written word can invoke all of human experience – every emotion, every faculty. The perceived image of film is finite, yet the images conjured by language – words – are fluid and illimitable, provocatively sensual.

So what is the future of the novel? Many writers and readers alike think the death knell is already being tolled. Because we live in such accelerated time, fewer people are buying books. It takes time to read a book; days, weeks, even months. A movie, however, can be taken in a single bite: two hours at most.

So often, people say to me, when they learn I'm a writer, 'Oh, I wish I read more, but I haven't got the time. I used to read when I was younger, but now...' Shrug.

I want to scream, then make time! I will defend the written word, but this is not an apologia.

I love movies. I love good movies, and even a few bad ones. I love the imagery, the director's vision. We all have our favourite directors. Scott, Cameron, Greenaway, Cronenberg, Jarman. I love animation: Brothers Quay, Svenkmajer, Anderson. But it is a different pleasure entirely from reading. In picking up a novel, the reader becomes its conspirator. For every person who reads the book, a new novel is created, because the story is visualised by the individual brain of the reader. It's true that publishers are producing more books now than they ever did, but concurrently, book sales are down, and library issues decline with each year that passes. More authors are being published, yes, but the print run numbers are lower, books have the average shelf life of a magazine in book shops, and writers cannot expect to earn a living wage from their work, unless, oh yes unless, they're prepared to be part of the pulp fiction stable. Naturally, there are always exceptions to this, and a number of good writers are also successful writers, but nowadays the terms are not mutually exclusive.

Market-force thinking has also affected film-makers, as funding is cut back, and directed towards mass market action films. Mercifully, there are still diamonds among the trash, and film-makers with vision and imagination are still able to produce lasting and thought-provoking films, but for every 'Orlando', there are two dozen 'Kindergarten Cops'.

So, is there a solution to this impasse? Short-term, it would not seem so. For writers, musicians and film-makers alike, the whole problem hangs upon the bones of the demon 'money'. We need another artistic revolution, where everyone is fired up enough to revolt against the Mammonistic greed of those who control the industries, and for people to invest in 'small label independents' once more. Those who run the publishing houses, (and record labels), should ideally be people who love books (and music), not the shark-eyed soulless who are out only to make a fast buck.

I find myself wondering whether, in fact, we the artists have also been subtly spellbound by the creed that we should create in order to make money. As I sit at my computer, weighed down with the burden of debt, sporadic income and piffling advances, I often consider prostituting my ability and rattling off a trash novel. I'm sitting there staring at the monitor, as I painfully extrude words from my soul, thinking 'why am I doing this?' The answer of course, as I'm sure it is for most creative people, is because for me writing is a compulsion, a tic, an ingrained habit. Even if I never sold another book, I'd have to write. So, with this diagnosis, how can writers, and other artists, face the future optimistically? What can we do to keep art alive, to feed it as it passes through what we can only hope is a temporary famine?

If reality is the construct of society, perhaps we only need to realign our perceptions in order to precipitate change. We do not need to rush through life as if the Hounds of Hell were on our heels; we can make time, simply by making the decision to do so. As a writer, I shall continue to climb slowly up the jagged rock faces of my own creations. I will take pleasure in the protracted act of it, I shall breathe deeply of the air at every level of the climb, observe the surroundings with patience and an open mind. I shall not be slave to those who have the power to pay me for my art; I will not let them take the pleasure of creating away from me.

Magazines and pundits are claiming that the advent of virtual reality is just another nail in the coffin for fiction, but only if the spirit of fiction is actually inside the coffin. Listen, I know where you can find the ultimate in virtual reality. It is with you already. Put on your favourite music, sit down with a book, open the first page, and begin to read. The journey might take weeks, and you will slip in and out of that virtual world with the simple act of picking up and putting down the book, but the journey will be yours alone. Sit down to the feast.

My Life as a Writer

Feature for 'Burn'
3rd August 2000

You know you're a professional writer when you've just read the most spiteful review of your career and then have to sit down and compose a feature encouraging and inspiring new writers in the field.

It never gets any easier trying to maintain some distance from unconstructive criticism, but there are compensations to help you through. You have to remember the thrill of when ideas come to you – at quiet moments of the day or before you go to sleep – and characters come alive to your inner eye, in rolling landscapes that spread before you waiting to be discovered. That is the essence of being a writer – not hair-pulling before an empty page or worrying about what other people might think of your words. The moment of pure creation remains forever unsullied and forever gives sustenance.

I'm often asked how you should go about coming up with ideas and plots for a first novel, and my advice remains the same as it always has. The first novel you write should be the one you've always wanted to read and have never found. It should be your dream book. This was certainly how I felt about my first novel, *The Enchantments of Flesh and Spirit*, which was the first book of the Wraeththu trilogy. Looking back on it now, I can see the flaws of inexperience in the writing, but I'm always made wistful by the innocence that shines from those pages. I wrote from the heart, ignorant of a future audience or criticism. It was free and unconstrained – something that rarely happens now. I don't think it's possible to hang on to that innocence, which is why the writing of a first novel is so precious and should be savoured – dry periods and all. The experience changes after first publication, and although it can become richer and more fulfilling in many other ways, a kind of free, childlike spontaneity is lost.

I suppose I always suspected, even if I never consciously examined it, that I was establishing future difficulties for myself in the kind of material I first chose to write. The Wraeththu books, for all their moments of wobbly plotting, were ground-breaking for their time. I was lucky in that my then publishers, Macdonald Futura, and my editor, the late Richard Evans, were prepared to take a risk with me.

I had lived with the idea of the Wraeththu for nearly ten years before I actually wrote anything down in coherent form. I'd dreamed up a post-holocaust kind of world, peopled by hermaphroditic beings, which by the time I came to write about it was very much inspired by the music scene I was involved in. This was Goth of the early Eighties, which was a flamboyant and playful arena, heavily influenced by the gay scene that educated the less extrovert in the excesses of outrageous dress and behaviour. The Wraeththu novels were unashamedly sexy, and ignored the accepted principles and rules of both science fiction and fantasy (as well as English language in some respects, but – well – I was young!), which didn't sit comfortably with many genre readers and critics, and the kind of sex involved wasn't the norm for SF or fantasy of that time. I was attacked from so many different directions, it was impossible to duck the missiles, but simultaneously I gained a loyal readership and a measure of staunch support from established writers. Getting published was, for me, the easy part. It was what came after that was more difficult. People either loved or hated what I did – and that's something that hasn't changed!

In the early days of my career, I gained a kind of notoriety for frequenting SF and fantasy conventions with what was usually referred to as an 'entourage', who were actually a group of my close friends – musicians and artists I lived and worked with. Conventions were alien territory to me. I felt like a rather over-fluffed peacock in an aviary of resentful sparrows. The peacock behaviour is all very well in a room full of like creatures but, if caught alone, the colourful bird tends to get pecked to death by birds of less gaudy plumage. So, I took some other peacocks with me. My friends, on the other hand, were intrigued by the whole thing and, if the truth be known, probably wanted to come along and create a bit of a stir. We had a lot of fun, but I suspect we were regarded as a bunch of attention-seeking upstarts by regular con-goers.

My desire to challenge fought constantly with the conditioned need to be liked and accepted. Unfortunately, the two do not exactly go hand in hand, and it took a long time and a lot of self-examination to rise above the negative aspects. The way I looked – heavy Goth trappings – influenced what people thought of both me and my work. In fact, the novels were probably judged many times merely by my personal appearance. What barely caused a blink in musical circles was regarded in a very different way in the world of SF and fantasy. No doubt many people thought it was just a gimmick designed to attract attention among competitors and that someone who dressed like me must be frivolous and shallow, and couldn't possibly be a 'real' writer. I was one of a kind – or at least if there were then any other 'alternative' genre writers they kept away from conventions and social events. I found people's attitudes amusing, hurtful and derisory by turn. It was difficult to be taken seriously – but fortunately not by readers. Appreciative readers are the life-blood for writers in what has become an extremely competitive and cutthroat industry. Happily, there are now a lot of writers who have emerged from various sub-cultures and the music scene, so their appearance at events doesn't raise quite as many eyebrows as it used to do.

Most genre writers come to publication through the route of having written lots of short stories or articles for SF and fantasy magazines. They make contacts at conventions and other events, and eventually, if all goes well, they find a home for a longer piece of work. By this time, they'll know a lot about the scene and how it works. I knew nothing about it. A series of coincidences propelled my synopsis for the Wraeththu trilogy into the right hands at the right time, but even then I knew this was not the usual way things went.

Although I had written stories all my life, it wasn't until I was twenty-six that I decided I hated working nine to five, and having wasted my educational years in questionable recreational activities, now needed to change tack with no qualifications to speak of. So, I set about writing the Wraeththu novel I'd been planning since I was about seventeen. My boyfriend at the time was in a band, and most of its members and the manager lived with us in the house I'd recently bought. One day, I went to Andromeda book shop in Birmingham, accompanied by Dave, the band's manager. He'd been encouraging me to write seriously and now took a hand in things by enquiring at the counter about how to get a genre book published. To cut a long story short, it so happened that Roy Wood, a rep from Futura, was in the shop at the time and was intrigued by the way Dave described my work. Roy then took up the cause and showed a copy of my synopsis and some sample chapters to Richard Evans at McDonald Futura. Richard wanted to see the rest of the book, and then, fortune of all fortunes, asked to buy it. This was a dream come true. I imagined there would be no looking back, but the reality was somewhat different. I had to face the fact that I wasn't destined by default to become rich overnight, but would have to slog long and hard for years to establish myself. I was dumped into an unknown and often hostile jungle, surrounded by strangers, some of whom were interested enough to get to know me and be supportive, while others barely bothered to hide their gibbering suspicion and dislike. I had to fight my way through this jungle, tripping up continually, learning hard lessons. But one day I found myself in a clearing and realised I knew the territory. I'd learned the language and the currency.

These experiences were the driving force behind my desire to help and encourage other new writers. A lot of the correspondence I received over the years was from people wanting to break into writing and who were seeking advice. I'm sure that many writers' first instinct to this request is to cry a jaded, 'Don't bother!', and mine was no different, but of course this is useless, because if writing is in a person's blood, they'll carry on doing it regardless of the pit traps awaiting them. I heard from young writers who didn't want to rehash tired old genre clichés, but were striving to create something new, to take fantasy into uncharted territory. I empathised with this entirely. For too long genre fiction has been regarded as pulp rubbish by the mainstream because it is judged by its worst examples. Newspapers, for instance, will not review it on principle, so a genre writer cannot expect to get the essential exposure a mainstream author will. Writing fantasy, horror and science fiction really does have to be a labour of love – although there are exceptions to the rule in the minority of writers, such as Pratchett, Eddings, King and Gemmell, who have managed to achieve prominence in the mainstream charts. Disheartening as it may sound, only 5% of writers earn their full living from writing. But, if you want to be one of that 5%, then I believe determination and persistence will get you there. The important thing is to believe in what you do and write to the best of your ability, accepting that you will never stop learning. To honour your work, and the creative principle behind it, write with integrity.

I have always written with integrity. Every novel is, to me, a magical working, permeated with the virtue of my craft. I have taken it upon myself to learn more about language and how it works, to refine my technique. Although what I have to say might not be what everyone wants to hear, I cannot write simply to appease. I cannot write safely. I write for myself and those who are open to my ideas, who might even share them. Many times, friends have said to me that I could perhaps be more successful if I did write something more conventional, but it's just not in me.

I think it's important that writers should try to overcome the competitive aspects of the industry and work together in some respects. Of course, you know that your first novel inevitably competes with hundreds of others at the same time, and the trick is to present yourself and your work to publishers as the best they can possibly buy. That means other writers have to be shouldered aside in the scrum. Also, it's difficult to maintain your position even once you've acquired that heady first sale. The pressure then mounts up for you to produce work regularly – preferably a novel a year, sometimes more. I've heard of writers, who you'd imagine were well-established, getting fed up with the whole thing and abandoning their writing careers. The trouble is you get very little support. Books on writing can help, but it's not the same as getting feedback.

A writer's working life is by necessity a lonely one. Unless you're collaborating with someone, you're not part of a team. You have to judge your own work objectively – and editing is a separate skill to writing. Once you've sold a book, you obviously acquire a professional editor, but unless you can hone your material to a presentable degree beforehand, it lessens the chances of a publisher wanting it. Chaotic narrative structure, meandering dialogue, clunky plotting and ill-formed background material can stifle the best story idea in the world. Editors nowadays do not have as much time for hands-on work as they did when I was first published. They can't nurture prospective talent as much. It's becoming rarer for editors to actually sit down with their writers and go through manuscripts page by page, pointing out weak areas, indicating strengths that should be built upon. This is not because editors care less than they used to, but that the industry has changed with the times and the editors now have more manuscripts to manage and more business tasks to take care of.

Working alone also means you have to impose strict

discipline upon yourself – which many writers find difficult. Writing to deadlines can either be terrifying or the only thing that gets you to work, depending on the individual. As a writer, you'll have no one in the room to share work gripes with, or who knows the job better than you do and can answer technical questions. Neither is there anyone experienced there to help out when your creativity grinds to a halt.

I realised that experienced writers can provide assistance and support for newcomers in all of these areas – simultaneously fulfilling part of the role that the old-fashioned editor used to do, while offering something more.

The idea for the fiction magazine *Visionary Tongue* came about when the band I was managing, 'Empyrean', broke up. I'd enjoyed producing their fanzine and thought about what I could do that was similar. My friend, Louise Coquio, was also interested in starting up a small press magazine and between us, we came up with the idea of a fiction zine with a difference. We would not only publish genre stories, but would enlist a team of professional writers as editors, who could work on a one to one basis with contributors, passing on their experience. The first issue appeared about five years ago, (1995), launched at the convention 'Welcome to my Nightmare' in Swansea. For the first issue, Lou and I did all the editing, but we ran about the convention press-ganging other writers to join us. The initial line up was Christopher Fowler, Graham Joyce, Kim Newman, Brian Stableford and Freda Warrington. As time went on, others joined, while a couple of the original editors dropped out because of heavy work commitments. Chris, Graham, Brian and Freda stayed with us throughout.

We produced thirteen issues of the magazine, but Lou and I eventually found it increasingly difficult to cope with. Initially, we had a team of helpers, who assisted one day a week with typing, photocopying, addressing mounds of envelopes and other general administration tasks. Unfortunately, they all had to give it up, one by one, as they moved away, started university courses, or got new jobs. Lou and I found the zine eating into more and more of our working time (we were collaborating on the non-fiction book *Bast and Sekhmet* then) and the high leasing cost of the professional standard photocopier wasn't covered by our sales. We realised a change was in order. One of our helpers, Si Beal, had moved away to take up a web design job, but was happy to turn VT into a webzine in his spare time, which meant we could still carry on with the original idea, but without all the paper work. Running it as a webzine would also mean we could take longer stories – the word count limit for the printed zine was about 3000 words, because of restrictions on the amount of pages. Originally, we aimed to publish about eight to twelve stories per issue, plus poems and illustrations. Now, we can take pieces of up to 30,000 words if necessary. One of the first stories we'd received for VT was *Heliotrope*, from Justina Robson, who is now a published author. Lou and I loved the story, but it was way too long for us. We had great pleasure in asking Justina if we could put it on the first 'edition' of the web site. Justina rewrote it for us – it was five years old by this time – and also became one of our editors.

One of the most satisfying things about working on VT was seeing so many of our contributors go on to publish novels, and further stories in professional magazines and short story anthologies. We don't take the entire credit for this, of course, as these were talented people who would eventually have been published regardless, but we do hope that their experience of working with a professional writer gave them a few stepping stones along the way. You can't help but feel a personal connection to an author with whom you've corresponded in depth about their work. Sometimes, stories can fly back and forth in email half a dozen times before they're ready for publication. Therefore, the successes of writers like Val Palmer, Tim Lebbon and Katherine Roberts brings a kind of parental glow to the heart.

VT is still going strong, even though we now have a much

smaller editorial team, consisting of Justina, Freda, Lou and myself. Given the changes in the zine, this works fine, as there is not so much pressure to edit lots of stories in a short time. All contributions are welcome, but I recommend prospective contributors take a look at the site first, to see what kind of material we take.

As well as working on VT, I've also run creative writing workshops. The first was at the local further education college. One of the things that struck me about the students was how many prospective writers didn't read. Also, a high percentage of them had no idea about how to use language. Grammar and syntax meant nothing to them. I'd initially had a rosy idea of all these creative types getting together once a week, where they'd all swap their stories and edit each other's work. While this was going on, I'd sit with a different student each week at the front of the class, working with them personally on one of their stories. Then, we'd have a session of the stories being read aloud, so the whole class could discuss the merits and downfalls of each piece. This, to me, was what the concept of 'workshop' meant. I quickly realised this was impossible – at least at the beginning.

For a start, people would regularly turn up with no work to be workshopped. Then, the standard of the work that did appear was sometimes so dodgy it couldn't even *be* workshopped but needed to be entirely rewritten. Therefore, I junked the rosy idea and began work in earnest on the mechanics of writing, giving lectures on narrative structure, syntax, rhythm, dialogue, grammar and punctuation. At the end of each lecture I'd devise exercises for the students to test what they'd learned, and also produced hand-outs (at great time and expense of my own, I might add, for which the college did not pay me) so that the students had material they could refer to at home, if necessary, while they were writing. I asked writer friends to come and talk to the group about their careers, and encouraged the students to read voraciously, not as readers, but as writers – which is very different. I also stressed the importance of actually producing work at home. It was not enough just to turn up once a week and expect to sit in class and write. There would be no time for interaction and discussion then. I realised I wasn't running a workshop, but a course. But again, the satisfaction of seeing progress in the students offset the niggles. One of my best students became a friend – Sian Kingstone. I also met Si Beal, now VT's web master, through the class.

The workshop folded a couple of years ago, due to bureaucratic changes in the further education system. The college wanted me to undergo proper teacher training, acquire a certificate, then run bona fide courses, which would have some kind of exam at the end. This was all very well, but it didn't accommodate those students who came back year after year, who saw the class as a social event as much as a learning process, and who would not want to go over the same material every year. So, I realised it was time for me to bow out. I ran a class at home for a year or so, but folded it when the majority of students had moved away from the area or acquired new commitments that meant they couldn't make the meetings.

Workshopping is, I think, an extremely valuable tool for writers, and compensates for the necessity of having to work alone. I recommend that if you're a writer who doesn't have a suitable group in your area, then start one. No matter what stage of expertise you are at yourself, you learn a great deal from editing other people's work. It's so much easier to spot mistakes in another writer's story than in your own, mainly because you have a distance from it. It's important to be able to take constructive criticism without getting upset and to give it sensitively. Writing is a very personal experience and an attack on someone's words can feel like an attack on themselves.

A feel for grammar and syntax often comes naturally to a born story-teller, but it never does any harm to brush up on the mechanics. The book I'd recommend to any writer is *The Way to*

Write by John Fairfax and John Moat (Elm Tree Books, 1981). This became the bible for my writing classes, and it taught me a great deal, even though I'd then been writing professionally for about ten years! I don't know if it's still in print, but book clubs such as The Softback Preview were offering it a few years ago. For those with internet access, perhaps Amazon.co.uk can supply it, or else do a search on a site like Bookfinder.com, which tries to locate second hand and/or out of print books. If all else fails, try the library request system! A good book on grammar is also useful. Another bible I recommend is the very wittily written *The Transitive Vampire: an Adult Guide to Grammar*, by Karen Gordon (Severn House, 1985). Again, this is probably long out of print, but well worth acquiring if you can. A writing group can share the cost of buying useful reference books, (taking turns to buy certain volumes), then swap them among members. Of course, it would be entirely illegal of me to say that if you do manage to get a useful out of print reference book from the library, you can always photocopy it, as it's worth the expense, because this would infringe copyright laws. So I won't.

Many of my students wanted to send their material off to publishers before they'd finished it, because they'd heard of how books can be commissioned from synopses and sample chapters. This is generally the case once you've established yourself, but for the first novel you really have to prove to potential publishers not only that you can write but that you can carry an idea to its conclusion in a full length work. Therefore, I always advise that you finish your first novel before trying to sell it. You should get several trustworthy people to read it and give you their comments (this is obviously where a writing group comes in handy, as other writers are more qualified to comment than anyone else). Once you've considered the remarks of your unofficial editors and have made any amendments to the manuscript as you see fit, then is the time to start sending it out.

Much of what follows is pretty bog standard information, but I'll include it for the benefit of anyone who doesn't know it.

First, make sure the manuscript conforms to what publishers like to see: double line space, on A4 paper, with 1" margins, with numbered pages. I always put my surname and the title of the book in the header of the pages, just in case any of them get separated from the main work. Create a neat title page, showing the book's name, your name, the word length and your address, phone number, and email address if you have one.

Get a copy of the *Writers and Artists Yearbook* or *The Writers' Handbook*, either of which list all UK publishers and agents. You have to compile a list of the most suitable houses for your book. It hardly needs to be said, but there's no point sending a horror novel to a publisher that specialises in romances or academic non-fiction. You can look at the publishers of books that are similar to yours to help make your choices.

There are two ways of going about submitting work. You can send a few sample chapters, a synopsis and a page of auto-biography, along with a covering letter to indicate that the rest of the book is available should the editor wish to see it. Or, you can send the whole thing out with the biog. and synopsis. There are arguments for and against both methods, so it's really up to you. Obviously, it's more economical not to keep printing out big manuscripts, and submitting a fragmenting, dog-eared manuscript to one publisher after another is definitely not to be recommended.

Should you receive a rejection, weep and rant only for a short while, then bear in mind that many successful authors were rejected dozens of times before their first book found the right home. Agatha Christie, for example, was rejected seventy times. Once you've recovered your composure, send the manuscript to the next name on your list.

There is also the question of agents. An agent is really essential once you begin to sell your work, but as an editor of mine once said to me, new writers might as well be sending their first novel to publishers as to agents. Once you've got an editor interested, it will be far easier to secure an agent to haggle over the contract. But, on the other hand, it is said that editors tend to take solicited work (i.e. represented) more seriously than manuscripts that are sent in by the authors themselves. This is a decision individual writers have to make for themselves. So, the best advice I can give is: go with your guts.

Once the magical event happens, and you get that phone call, email or letter with positive news, you can expect to have to make at least some changes to the book. First, the editor themselves will offer a critique. Sometimes, the editorial might be a dozen pages long, which can look depressing. But I've rarely disagreed with anything an editor's said to me, so I think you just have to grit your teeth and sit down to sort out the glitches. Once the editor is happy with it, the manuscript will be sent to a copy editor, who will then correct all your grammar, spelling and punctuation. Copy editors sometimes meddle with the actual content of the book too. Again, I've rarely had bad experiences from them, and most are blessedly thorough, spotting plot errors and anachronisms I've missed, even though I've read the book dozens of times. But as far as grammar's concerned, sometimes the copy editor will change the text to conform to a particular style, when the original text is not exactly wrong. You can always argue the point about this if it really bothers you.

The final stage is reading through your book in proof form to check for any final typos or errors before it's printed up.

Then, it's publication day and out comes the champagne. After that heady experience – and it should be enjoyed with abandon – you have to deal with the realities of being a published writer. It might not have occurred to you before (it didn't to me), but now you have an audience, and part of that audience inevitably includes critics. This leads back to the beginning of this feature. The well-known adage 'there's no such thing as bad publicity' is really no comfort when your baby has just been savaged in print. You can get a dozen rave reviews, but I guarantee the one that will stick in your mind and worry you into the night is the lone bad one. There's no point in me saying you have to develop a thick skin and shrug such things off. Mostly, they will continue to hurt, even if you write professionally for fifty years! You haven't spent a year of your life, perhaps writing around a gruelling day job, just for some hack to dismiss your labour of love with a few snide words. The best thing to remember is that a review is in print for at best a month, while your book will hopefully be around for years to come, as a well-thumbed copy on readers' book-shelves, or even better as a reprint. Sometimes, galling as it may be, even the bitchiest of critics have something useful to say. Other times, you will fume impotently, because it's patently obvious the reviewer hasn't even read the book properly or at least has failed to pick up on your intentions. One thing I can't stress too strongly though: *never* respond personally to a bad review. The editor of the publication will inevitably give the reviewer the last word on the subject and you just come across as peevish and undignified. After a few weeks, the sting of the criticism will fade and hopefully you'll have received some nice fan letters in the meantime to make you feel better.

So that about wraps up the Constantine thoughts on how to get a book published and how to cope with it all once you've done it. Good luck with all your endeavours!

How Do I Get a Fantasy Book Published?

Immanion Press Author Information Article

As with previous articles I've written concerning getting a book published, times have moved on since I wrote the few that follow here. Most of my writing articles are over ten years old now, but apart from the impact of technology on the actual submission process, the advice otherwise remains the same. Nowadays, many publishers will take – or even prefer to take – electronic submissions, rather than printed manuscripts. All publishers have web sites with submission guidelines on them.

I'm sure that every published writer would say that they are asked this question more often than any other. There are plenty of books available that give advice on the subject, including such worthy tomes as *The Writers' Handbook* and *The Writers and Artists' Year Book*, as well as a multitude of self-help titles. There are also many web sites that will offer you information. But do these guarantee you the ability to write a best-seller?

It has to be said that a lot of it is down to luck. You might have the most saleable idea in the world, but unless it falls on the right desk at the right time, it might as well not exist. Occasionally, the publishing industry tends to get all hysterical about a new manuscript, and whoever ends up buying it will publicise it to the hilt. This is generally necessary, for any auction situation means they probably had to pay big money for it, in which case the only way to recoup is to actually market the product. It's a well-known fact, especially in genre fiction, that the advance directly affects the publicity budget. If you sell your first book for a pittance, you shouldn't expect to have adverts on the Tube for it. In fact, your publicity budget will be minuscule, if it exists at all. Unfortunately, unless it's crazy season, you'll probably get an advance that seems risible in comparison to the amount of work hours that went into the book. It's tough and demoralising, but you have to remember that publishing is a business and works like any other. The norm is that new writers get small advances, and build up slowly, as they build up their readership. And the majority of promotion will be down to you. Just because you're a writer, you're no more privileged or entitled to special treatment than any other person who has a product to sell. That's point number one. But some authors are still selling their first books for big money, so maybe we have to analyse what gets the industry hot.

(One thing worth mentioning here is that J K Rowling's first Harry Potter book was turned down by two publishers before being taken on by Bloomsbury. Imagine how she felt when those rejections came in and how she must feel now. Take heart. You can get lucky.)

Agents and editors will tell you that publishers are always looking for new angles on fantasy. It may come as surprise news to most people who browse bookshops, where there is little evidence of originality, but this is what I'm told. And happily there will always be exceptional new books coming out; even if the majority of new titles in shops seem fairly run of the mill. If you're working on your own first novel, it's a good idea to read the best new titles, not just to size up the competition but also to analyse what makes the books different from the rest. Point number two. An author should read as a writer not as a reader. There is a difference.

A way to strive for originality is to avoid traditional fantasy tropes. I've seen too many manuscripts telling stories about elves and orcs or vampires, which have all been done to death – or undeath as the case may be. What you should seek is a new vein to tap. Every country in the world has a rich, ancient mythology, some of which has barely been acknowledged in fantasy fiction. Celtic and Norse mythology are common, as is

Native American, and books influenced by Japanese and Chinese cultures have appeared, but what about the rest of the world? If this approach attracts you, get a good encyclopaedia of mythology and start looking. The myths themselves can generate ideas for novels and stories. If you really must have characters as elves and orcs, at least try to come up with new terms for them, and do something different with them.

The best novels come from intertwining plot strands, so it's a good idea to jot down several myths, then combine and change them to come up with something unique. For many writers, the first novel derives from a compulsion, so you generally know what you're going to write from the start, but if you can stand back and regard your idea critically and think it might be a tad derivative, keep the plot and characters, but tinker with the 'dressing'. Guard against mixing cultures though. I once read a novel that featured deities and beliefs from both Celtic and Egyptian traditions, all mixed up together, and it wasn't very convincing.

It's unlikely that a publisher would commission a novel from synopsis by a first time author, so the next thing you need to do is write the bulk of the book. It's feasible you could sell it with 200 strong pages or so, but I'd recommend getting it all down, at least in first draft.

Despite what I said above about the compulsive nature of writers, some people have asked me: what should I write for my first novel? How can I come up with an idea? If you want to write, but haven't been 'possessed' (and that is what it can feel like) by an idea, the answer is simple. Your first novel should be the book you've always wanted to read but have never found. Writing can be an academic exercise, but novels that truly touch the heart of a reader are those with spirit and feeling. That has to come from love. Your first novel is a love affair with your creativity. Although subsequent books can be equally fulfilling, nothing compares with the first one, the first love.

So when the bulk of your book is written, what comes next?

The answer is something that many people find difficult to tackle: the synopsis.

The synopsis is effectively the advert for your book. It's what potential publishers look at first and they have to be intrigued enough by it to want to read some of the actual manuscript. The problem is that all the complexities of plot and characterisation are very difficult to capture in a short précis. When the story is set down in its bare bones, so to speak, it can appear flat and uninspiring compared with the real thing. So you have to go for a punchy approach, writing the synopsis as if it was the one thing that will attract people to buy and read your book. I wouldn't go so far as to say it should be like an extended cover blurb, but it should have the same direct and immediate feel. There should be no flab or extended rambling, just get to the point. It's not an exercise to prove to publishers that you can write beautifully. It's a sales device. Really, it requires a distinctly separate skill to that of writing fiction, so if you know anyone in the advertising industry, who can give you a hand, ask them for help. Remember that editors receive hundreds of submissions a week, so what's important is that you convince them your book is much better and more original than anything else coming their way.

Another problem with this is that many writers are naturally self-effacing and it really makes them squirm to promote themselves in a self-aggrandising manner. That's why it often helps to get someone else to assist you, who you can trust. They won't be as sensitive about it as you are.

Once you have a synopsis that you think does the business, start sending it out to publishers with a covering letter, about a page of biographical material (again, punchy and interesting), and a chunk of manuscript. It hardly needs to be said, but it does help if your work is nicely presented. The manuscript should always be double line spaced, with 1″ margins all round, and the pages should be numbered.

There are arguments for and against trying to secure an

agent before you send work to publishers. Obviously, an agent will represent you better than you can represent yourself, and they lend the work an air of respectability, in that it has already passed some kind of test for them to want to represent it. However, one editor of mine said she thought that if authors are sending work to agents they might as well be sending it to editors. The main concern with this is the aforementioned glut of unsolicited (i.e. unrepresented) manuscripts with which editors are deluged continually. Perhaps it is better to give your book the best possible chance and try to get an agent first. It is really up to you.

It can help if you've already made forays into the genre by selling short stories to magazines or having them accepted for fantasy web zines. This gives you a writing CV.

So, if you're lucky enough to find a home for your masterwork, what can you expect? At first, it's a dizzying experience. Suddenly, you're a kind of celebrity and that can feel extremely strange. However, once the champagne's run dry and you've fluttered back down to earth, you have to carry on working. It's unlikely (unless you're a literary genius) that you won't have to make amendments to your novel once it's been accepted. If you get a good editor – and thankfully there are still many good editors out there – they'll help you craft your work to make it better and stronger. One thing I can't stress too strongly: don't be precious about what you write. If you're prepared to accept constructive criticism, your life will be a lot easier. Just remember that editors aren't trying to attack you personally: they simply want the best for your book. So it's pointless getting upset and annoyed when they suggest changes, even if those changes seem radical. You have to trust that they know what they're talking about. It would only reflect badly on them if a book they've promoted as the next big thing is savaged by critics. I know the arguments. As an editor myself, I've heard them a hundred times. 'This is *my* work, my lifeblood, the outpourings of my soul! How can you want to change it? This is what I've written. This is how it is!'

Well, all right, but do you actually want to sell the book? If you feel a word of it can't be touched, perhaps it belongs in your diary rather than a bookshop. As I said before, writing is an industry and temperament can't come into it.

Hard as it sounds, you should look upon your novel – no matter how beloved – as a product. To be a professional writer, your product has to sell. Aside, perhaps, from independent publishers like Immanion Press and our kind, the people who run publishing (as opposed to editors) aren't in it solely for love of books. In the case of big publishers especially, they're in it to make profits. If they didn't make profits, they couldn't publish books. When you've got the writing bug, and stories seem to flow through your very veins, so that your only purpose in life is to express them, this hard, unpalatable truth can come like a punch to the gut. But you can't ignore it. Once you've accepted it and thought, 'Oh well, that's just the way it is', you can shrug it off and get on with being creative. In real terms, the only time you have to deal with it is when you're actually selling new work or when your book comes out. The rest of the time you can forget about it, write and be happy.

The marvellous thing at the end of all this is that your book will eventually reach readers, and they care about books very much. Their support restores your faith in what you're doing. It's really sad that publishing has had to change from the gentle, scholarly profession it used to be, but we should look on the bright side and at least be grateful that it's still thriving.

Self Publishing:
the Pitfalls and the Promise

Immanion Press Author Information Article

As it becomes ever more difficult to get a foothold in the writing world, never mind sustain a comfortable living from it, many more young or novice writers are turning to self-publishing, so that their work can reach an audience. In some ways, this echoes the rebellious stance of the Punk era in the late Seventies, when a deluge of new bands - all attitude and safety pins - burst onto the scene, and small record labels sprouted up all over the place, eager to disseminate this snarling, spitting music around the country. That happened because the big labels had a stranglehold on music, and popular music itself had suffered for it, becoming largely stale and predictable.

Much the same could be said of standard publishing nowadays. Editors, seemingly held at gunpoint by paranoid accountants, are even less willing to take risks on new talent than in the past. Generally, the new writer finds themselves, armed only with their manuscripts, facing what appears to be a cyclopean, impregnable citadel, whose drawbridge is truly up. The other side of the coin is that new writers also come cheap. Suppose the drawbridge is lowered, and the author is taken into the citadel? All too often, they are grateful beyond words just to see their novels and stories in print, and any money earned from it seems like an unexpected bonus. It's great to be paid a little bit for indulging a 'hobby'. Most of us would continue to write regardless of whether we're published or not. However, the low advances offered for novels – and not just first novels nowadays – do nothing to help the situation for authors who see their writing as their vocation in life, and not simply something they do in their spare time after work. In addition, the advance of computer technology has made it far easier for people to produce manuscripts, regardless of talent and skill. Consequently, there is a never-ending supply of hopeful authors, few of whom can expect to find a publisher who is willing, if not able, to support and evolve their career in writing. It all comes down to commitment, and unfortunately even when an editor is committed to your work, those who control the purse strings might not be quite so accommodating. To become a big name, you have to be promoted and, as far as the accountants who now run publishing are concerned, to be promoted, you have to be a big name. Is it any wonder, then, that writers are sick of the situation, and think, 'stuff it, I'm going to do it myself'?

The relative cheapness of self-publishing via the internet has enabled many people to start their careers independent of a professional publisher. All you need is a decent understanding of basic book formatting and access to a cheap printing company (usually print on demand nowadays). You can try to get your book reviewed on any suitable web site or blog, persuade amenable local or specialist book shop proprietors to stock it, or advertise it on your personal web site, complete with text extracts and a glam author photo. In fact, you might not even bother with the hard copy printing stage, preferring to see your work as an electronic book, existing only in cyber-space. It's not the same as a printed artefact in your hand (that's irreplaceable!), but you might earn a little money from it, and at least people will have easy access to your work. So as you can see, it's not that difficult to become a published writer. Is this a good thing or a bad thing?

It has to be seen as beneficial for literature as a whole that new writers can find an outlet for their work, and that readers can have access to new talent and ideas they might otherwise be denied. Books that might never otherwise see the light of day, being indefinable in terms of genre, or too experimental in form, can reach an audience. I support self-publishing wholeheartedly in this respect, but just one thing niggles me, and it's quite a big 'one thing'.

The major benefit of being published by a professional publisher is that your work will be edited, polished to its (hopefully) full potential. An experienced editor can guide and teach new writers, pointing out the weaknesses in their work, playing up the strengths. All too often, the books I see that have been produced by enterprising free spirits fall down because the quality of the writing simply isn't good enough.

You make a decision to write a novel and turn on your computer. Your monitor blooms with a blank page, the cursor is blinking expectantly, waiting for you to begin. Your head is full of ideas, characters are straining at the leash to be released onto the page, plots twirl and plait in your mind, landscapes are ready to pour out of your fingers. So, you crack your knuckles and you're off.

In the fullness of time, you will have completed your opus, and will be ready to have it printed, one way or another. Of course, for most of us, the process isn't quite that painless, but sooner or later, the book or stories will be finished. You might have rewritten it/them several times, or given copies to your friends to read and criticise. Some people might have come back with helpful comments, which you may or may not have taken on board. But ultimately, only *you* decide when that work is ready to be printed, and from what I've seen from self-published authors, this is sometimes too soon. And this is a shame, because in all too many instances, the problem isn't lack of talent, but lack of skill and experience.

As writers, we have to develop an 'ear': for words, for meaning, for the music and colour of our prose. We have to learn when to rein in our muse and when to let it go at a full gallop. We have to understand about narrative structure – what might seem the most basic of principles; a story has to have a beginning, middle and an end. We have to control our readers' eyes with the rhythm of our sentences, which involves knowing about good syntax, punctuation and pacing. This makes the difference between an easy read, when we're carried along by the fluidity of the prose, and a stultifying wade through a chaotic swamp of words. Too much exposition in the wrong place and readers get bored; too little and they feel short-changed in background and setting. Our characters have to be convincing, so that readers empathise with them. Our plot-lines must be trimmed of cliché. Dialogue should perform the dual task of expanding upon characterisation as well as move the story along. We also have to concern ourselves with viewpoint, and keep it consistent. The story itself should be credible and intriguing, so that our readers want to keep turning the page. Plot holes should be filled, chronology accurate. All loose ends have to be tied by the last page, and narrative clues inserted expertly and unobtrusively along the way. Writing and editing are two separate skills, but a self-published author has to be proficient at both.

A book was sent to me a while ago by a young writer, who had done an impressive job on the appearance of his first, self-published novel. The book was beautifully put together and, as an artefact, would shame no book shelf, but once I began to read it, discomfort slowly spread through me. Meaningless dialogue went on for pages at a time, and great clumps of extremely detailed description detracted from the thrust of the story. The grammar and punctuation wasn't that brilliant, which impeded easy reading, and the characterisation was hackneyed. The text was peppered with repetitious words and phrases. The novel just wasn't a page-turner; my interest quickly flagged. I could see that if an editor had worked with this writer, together they would have crafted a good first novel.

Copy editors are employed by publishers to polish up grammar and syntax in manuscripts, so some writers don't concern themselves greatly with this aspect. (Not an attitude I'd advocate, by the way!) But when you're self-publishing, it becomes of prime importance. The subject matter of the book

I've just mentioned – vampires – was popular, and so was the style in which it had been written or, more accurately, the style its author had striven for. But the execution of the idea let it down. That this novel was clearly a labour of love, into which its author had invested copious amounts of time, energy and money, made it difficult for me to criticise him. But this was not the worst example of a self-published novel I've ever seen.

There are many ways in which new writers can avoid some of the pitfalls of the self-published first novel or collection of stories. First, I would recommend joining a writers' workshop or creative writing course. The stereotype of this kind of group conjures images of elderly people who write twee poetry. I know that because it was an opinion I once held myself. Then I ended up teaching a creative writing course at the local college. The students came from a wide range of backgrounds and ages. Some were into genre fiction, some not, but on the whole, they all worked well together, pooling their strengths and learning from each other's mistakes and successes. However, if you really can't find a suitable group, start your own. I ran my class for several years, with new faces turning up every term, so I can promise you that you won't run out of candidates.

The most helpful groups are those where work is swapped between members for critical appraisal. You learn as much from editing someone else's work as you do from their assessment of yours. Somehow, it's always easier to spot mistakes and weaknesses in someone else's story. It's actually quite a big responsibility to heap onto a friend or family member when you ask them to read your manuscript for you. Are they really qualified to criticise constructively? The last thing you want is someone just handing it back to you with a nervous smile, saying, 'Yeah, that's great.' If they say that, you should want to know why it's great. Then ask about the weaknesses. Again, your volunteer might not have the terminology to explain what worked best for them and what didn't. They might also be worried about upsetting you. It's always preferable to get other writers to look at your work. You can guarantee you won't get a lukewarm response, even if they don't come out with what you want to hear.

Secondly, don't underestimate the worth of self-help books about writing. Some of them are extremely well-written, by successful authors, who pass on tips of the trade. Take time to learn about the technicalities of your craft – get a good book on grammar and punctuation. When you read other people's fiction, read it as a writer, not as a reader. Think about what made the book work for you, or why you didn't like it. Read lots. I used to be astounded when students turned up at my class and told me they didn't read much.

Of course, if you want to make a decent living from writing, it's unlikely self-publishing will answer your prayers, even if there are salient examples of success stories out there – the exception rather than the rule. However, a well-crafted, self-published first novel can only help you to sell future work to a publisher, especially if you can collect a few favourable reviews from magazines and review sites. Review copies are very important – send out as many as you can, especially to the bigger magazines and web/blog sites. Most bloggers now prefer PDFs of books to review, which helps keep costs low. Send copies to the British Science Fiction Association and The British Fantasy Society for their review magazines. (These examples, of course, are all UK-based genre publications concerned with fantasy, horror and sf. I'm sure every country has their equivalent.) In all cases, make it clear how much your publication costs, (including post and packing), and how people can order it. Design a page of biographical material, with an author photo. This is your self-promotion. Send it out with every book. Around twenty-five years ago, a friend of mine self-published to start with, and through sheer back-breaking effort shifted 20,000 copies of his first full-length book. (He'd already published quite a few pamphlets and chap-books.) It's a phenomenal amount, as most first authors could expect to feel inordinately successful if their book sold between 5,000–10,000. My friend sold so many copies because he drove around the country with his car full of books, persuading shops to stock it. This was way back before there was the internet to publicise your work. But it paid off for him and he eventually got contracts from big publishers and made a solid career from writing.

It's also vital to have a busy internet presence. That means having a web site and/or blog, and belonging to social media such as Facebook and Goodreads in order to promote your work. Join groups and add magazines, small presses and review sites to your friends' lists. Don't be afraid to self-publicise, because it's the only publicity you have. It costs nothing to promote yourself on the internet, so use it to its full potential. I'm sure you'll find many helpful articles if you do a search on self-promotion for self-published writers.

Persistence and determination are all-important, but so is talent and skill. Take the time to hone your work and learn about your craft. There are few easy routes to success, but if you give it your best, you'll get there in the end.

Making Your Writing Live

Immanion Press Author Information Article

New writers brim over with fantastic ideas for their stories and novels. The images live powerfully in their heads, and their task is to commit that strength and feeling to the printed page. But there can't be a writer alive who hasn't had to face the fact that their abstract images often lose something in the translation. The most brilliant ideas can seem flat and lifeless once they're written down. It takes practice and skill for a writer to be able to give the reader their vision, and the most powerful tool they have at their disposal is language itself.

Whole books have been written on the subject of how to write well, so it's impossible to impart all that information in a small article. However, I'll try to address some of the most important points.

A book is a form of virtual reality. Good writing carries the reader off into imaginary realms so cleverly that they forget they're reading. They're really there in that other world. The last thing a writer wants is for the reader to be jolted back to mundane reality. But this can happen. Awkward phrases can jar. Unlikely actions, reactions or speech from characters can shatter the suspension of disbelief. When you're reading a book, you don't have someone speaking aloud to you in a spooky voice. The words alone have to make you feel nervous or scared. I can remember being terrified by Stephen King's *The Shining* when I first read it. So how does a writer create this effect?

It's important you don't worry about syntax, or any other technical problem, until you've got your first draft down. Second and subsequent drafts are for grooming and polishing. Your first draft should be pure creativity, whether it's in good English or apparent Double Dutch.

I believe successful writing is the result of a combination of things, all of which are equally important, but I'll begin with syntax, or sentence construction. It might seem obvious, but sentences have to make sense. If a reader finds they're going back to read a sentence again, because they can't work out what the writer means, they'll remember they're only reading. The mood is lost. It's important to have the words and parts of a sentence in the right order. Again, this might seem obvious, but all too often, when working on novels from new writers, I read sentences along the lines of:

'Over the lazy dog the quick red fox jumps.'

The image this conjures in the reader's mind is muddled. Ok, we've got a lazy dog, we've got a quick red fox, but then the reader has to wait to see what happens.

'The quick red fox jumps over the lazy dog' presents the information in the right order. We see the fox, we see him jumping, and then we see what he jumps over. We haven't got the fox at a standstill, next to the dog, waiting to see the jump. The same could be said of the sentence 'the cow jumped over the moon', or 'red sky at night, shepherd's delight'. 'Over the moon the cow jumped' and 'shepherd's delight, red sky at night' don't convey the information in quite the same precise way.

Following on from syntax is pace, which we can regard as the partner of the former, because neither feels right unless they're together. The pace of your sentence does much to create a mood. You might use longer, more rambling sentences, with a string of sub-clauses, to describe an initial scene, or action when there's no particular sense of urgency or danger.

As an example, I'll quote from my novel *Scenting Hallowed Blood*. This is the beginning of the first paragraph of the book:

'He was little more than a boy, gleaming in the candle-light like an icon, while the night wind cleared its throat in the long, narrow chimneys of stone that threaded down from the cliff-top to the cave. Candles were set at his feet in a ring; rough wax obelisks, ill-formed as if shaped by hasty hands.'

I wanted the words to have a lilting rhythm, almost like poetry, to lull the reader. I didn't want their hearts beating faster at that point, although I planted narrative clues that something odd is about to happen with how I described the candles 'ill-formed as if shaped by hasty hands'. This was an urgent ritual. I wanted the reader to ask immediately: 'why?'

The sentence construction should become snappier, more abrupt, once the action begins to start. Here is a later extract from the same novel to illustrate the point:

'The ground rushed up to meet him, each detail of the rocks below brought into sharp focus. Nano-seconds stretched into eternity. He knew he was falling fast, yet it seemed to take forever to reach the ground. *I was tricked! I am dying!* The scapegoat. Pushed from the cliff. Panic surged through his body. Then the ground disappeared. He fell into a black abyss. Down. Down. Through time.

Another thing I did here was break a grammatical rule in using little bits of sentences called fragments, as in 'Down. Down. Through time' and 'Pushed from the cliff'.

Fragments can be used for dramatic effect in certain scenes.

Also, the choice of tenses and verb forms adds to the drama. For example, 'she was sitting on the battlements and she was howling', has far less drama and impact than the simple 'she sat on the battlements and howled.' A horror writer might even be tempted to use the construction of 'She sat on the battlements. She howled.'

Every word we know has associations connected with it. Even down to simple colours. For example, if someone says the word 'red', people might say it made them think of blood or danger. Similarly, blue might invoke the response of sea, sky or sadness. Therefore the words a writer chooses to use are very important. You want to invoke the right response in the reader. Good writing is precise and clear. Compare:

'It was a noise made by someone who was extremely frightened.'

To:

'It was a scream.'

Generally, in a piece of horror writing, you'd avoid soft, fluffy words. If you were describing a monster, for example, you might not want to say, 'It waddled towards me, a huge, pillowy mass...' The word 'waddle' conjures an image of something rather ludicrous and cumbersome, while 'pillowy' sounds like marshmallow. The reader might think 'that's not very scary. It wouldn't take much to run away from that'. Therefore, it might be better to say something like 'It lumbered towards me, a hideous amorphous mass...' Now a reader might worry about that creature.

Punctuation is also vitally important. It is the tool writers use to guide their reader's eyes along the text. If the sentences are badly constructed and punctuated, readers might be confused as to the meaning, and then they're back in mundane reality with a bump. You've lost them.

Take time to learn about punctuation and how it makes your reader speed up and slow down, and helps them navigate the winding paths of your work; these are road signs of writing. Each punctuation mark has a different 'weight'. A comma is far lighter than a full stop (or period), for example. Commas are slight pauses upon the path; a full stop makes you – stop.

Similarly, colons, semi-colons, ellipses, dashes and parentheses (brackets) all work to guide your reader's eye. Questions marks need no explanation. But be careful with exclamation marks – sloppy writers tend to over use them for emphasis when skilled word craft is preferable.

You will find web sites online that provide information and examples of all the tools of the writer's craft. Become proficient with the tools at your disposal and you'll be a better writer for it.

Pruning Your Work

Immanion Press Author Information Article

Most writers tend to fall into one of two categories: the under-writer and the over-writer. Let's call these the starveling and the bloater. The starveling produces bare, stark first drafts; there might only be slashes of dialogue without any 'stage directions' to show what the characters are doing, or hardly any description, or scant exposition. Some starvelings I know write first drafts that read like synopses. Their subsequent drafts involve adding all the extras – the ornaments, if you like – to the basic story. But this piece isn't about starvelings. Their problems will be discussed another time. No, this is for the bloaters among you!

Bloaters are greedy for words. Not for them the crisp-bread and Philadelphia Lite of first drafts. They often say the same thing over and over, but in slightly different ways. The trouble is, when the words are pouring out and some of those sentences are just so tasty, they seem too good to waste. Bloaters might go over the top with description. Disciplined descriptive detail makes for good story-telling, but too much of it gets in the way of the story. Readers get bored and lose interest.

Sometimes, when you're writing, it's easy to include dialogue and description – even whole scenes – that have little or no bearing on pushing the story forward. In later drafts, all that can go. But the problem is, when you're so close to a piece of work, it's often difficult to determine exactly what's essential and what isn't. After all, the story is a virtual living world in your imagination. You know everything about it and you want your readers to share that experience. Cutting too much might damage that vision. In a full length novel, it isn't always necessary to junk all the sub-plots and 'asides'. They can enrich the story rather than hamper it. The trick is to achieve a balance.

It's important to remember that the short story and the novel are very different animals. You have to be much stricter with yourself about extraneous detail in a short story, which should be as polished and perfect as you can get it. Editing and writing are two distinct skills. But despite this, I believe that all writers can train themselves to edit their own work to some extent. So, how do you start learning the skill?

It helps to get other people to look at your work, especially if they read a lot themselves. Tell them what you want them to look for, stressing you want an honest response – you won't bite their heads off if they come back with negative remarks. (That's something I could write another whole article on – accepting helpful criticism gracefully!) The main things for them to search for are repeated and unnecessary information. Once your readers have come back with their opinions, take a look at the story again. On your computer, create a copy of the story, make those cuts, print the piece out, and read it once more. Does the story work better now? Has the narrative flow improved without losing any of the atmosphere you set up?

Another helpful practice is to read your story aloud – you can be sure that repetitions and tedious sections will make their presence known. If you can, read to an audience of one or more – their comments will be helpful too.

The object of the exercise is to remove all information from the story that waylays the reader unnecessarily, that does nothing to progress the plot or plump up characterisation. It's often tempting to keep sections in, because you think they build a character up in the reader's mind. Pages of personal history about your protagonists might be useful as a reference source for you – but how much does the reader need to know for the story to work for them? Be severe with yourself here. Don't let your story get drowned by torrents of irrelevant personal detail.

It helps to try out different readers until you come across the one (or more) who seems to give the best advice; if you can join a writers' workshop or creative writing class, even better. (If there isn't one in your area, you could start one). This is because another good way to learn how to edit your own work is to edit other people's. It's surprising how much you can pick up from their mistakes.

Once you've found your unofficial editor, nine times out of ten their suggestions will bring unexpected new life to a story. I'm often amazed at how judicial cutting seems to electrify the prose, bringing everything into focus. Observing what other people regard as non-essential information helps train you to recognise it yourself.

Bloat notoriously shakes the meaning of a piece of text out of focus, such as when a writer says in twenty words what can easily be said in ten. I'm not talking about description here, (although that can suffer from bloat), but simple narrative. Most commonly, the problem manifests as an army of words that colonise your sentences, thereby obscuring the meaning and creating an area of mud in which the reader loses their footing.

Here's an example; a sentence from the original draft of a story, which once appeared in a magazine I edited. The protagonist is just taking a bite from a chicken leg. The original sentence read:

'Her jaws moved, but as far as she was concerned it was nothing more than an inedible pulp'.

There is a grammatical problem with this sentence too, but after he reworked the story, the author's final version read:

'Her jaws moved with effort.'

The reworded sentence conveys all the meaning of the first – she didn't really enjoy the meat – without all the padding. To keep more description, the sentence could also have been reworded as: 'Her jaws moved, but the meat was an inedible pulp in her mouth.' The wording is still more concise than in the original sentence and the meaning is clear.

A good exercise is to take a paragraph from one of your stories and chop it by half. Be harsh with yourself. This *is* just an exercise. Do it in three or four different ways. Cut different words. Reword sentences more concisely. But notice the effect on the whole.

An excess of unnecessary words might not be the problem. Perhaps you are one of those writers who must say everything at least twice. You think of one metaphor to describe the moonlight, you think of another. They both make your skin tingle, so both have to go in. As they're both so evocative and sensual, surely no-one will mind them being there? But there are hundreds of ways to describe something creatively – so why waste them all on one story? Again, learn to recognise when you're repeating yourself, and keep the repetitions in a separate file or on paper. Use them somewhere else, on their own, where they can shine like gems.

It took me over ten years of professional writing and fourteen novels to train myself to spot occasions of bloat. Even now, a great many years later, I don't notice them all, especially when I've just finished writing a novel or story, and I'm still too close to it. It's usually after a month or so, when the copy-edited manuscript comes back to me, that the repetitions, over-long descriptions and unnecessary details, scenes and dialogue leap from the page. My writing now is a lot more concise than it was. But one thing I have learned over the years: I don't expect my first, or even my second, drafts to be perfect. Criticising yourself too harshly at this early stage can lead to writer's block. There'll be plenty of time later to get out the polishing tools.

Writing can be a difficult process. The stories blossom in our minds, but when we sit down to commit them to screen or paper, the words often don't come out as scintillating as we imagined them – or worse, they refuse to come out at all. We have the vision in our minds, the essential feeling, but sometimes despair of capturing that in the written word. It's important to *just write*. Train yourself to think *as* you write rather than *before* you write. Editing a piece of work is the easy part, the enjoyable process of tinkering with the words.

Most of us are either starvelings or bloaters. Sometimes I'm one or the other. The main thing is learning the techniques of your craft, so you can polish your stories yourself.

Falling Standards in Writing

Blog Post Feb 2014

My own writing aside, I want to let off steam about something that's increasingly getting on my nerves: the poor standard of grammar, spelling, syntax and punctuation in so many of the published works I read, and also in magazines and newspapers, and even in broadcasting on the radio and television. Every editor, I'm sure, has pet hates. (I won't go into Ian Whates' long-standing war with the word 'it'!) Mine include the wrong use of verb forms, in particular the now all too common 'he was sat', 'she was stood' etc., instead of the correct forms of either 'she stood' or 'she was standing'. I'm reading a novel at the moment and am being tripped up and ejected from immersion in the story every few minutes by one of these appalling bloopers. Strangely, it's not consistent, and the author gets the verbs right as often as she gets them wrong. I can only assume she doesn't have a full knowledge of grammar and therefore lacks control of her prose. This particular, horrible corruption has crept into all aspects of the written and spoken word, and I really hate it. Whenever I see it I can't help thinking the writer is just lazy and uneducated in their craft.

Another pet hate, and I think this has come over to the UK from America, is the use of 'off of' for 'from', such as 'off of that programme on the telly', instead of 'from that programme on the telly'. It's forgivable in toddlers, i.e. people learning to talk, but not in adults, and certainly not in writers. I see this horror all over the place, and the mere sight of it is enough to raise my blood pressure! Call me a grammar Nazi if you like, but I really detest the sloppiness it reveals.

Another annoyance is misuse of the word 'that', when 'who' should be used, i.e. 'these are the people that were stood'…

oops, I mean, 'these are the people who were standing'! It's clear the writers concerned aren't aware that when it's a person or people we use 'who'; when it's an object or an animal, (and some writers might even contest the latter), we use 'that'.

I often see weak punctuation, syntax and spelling, as if the books I'm reading haven't been edited properly, if at all. I also see cases of endless repetitions of words and phrases close to each other on a page, (and not in a deliberate, poetic or dramatic way), which should be spotted by an editor, even if the writer is blind to them. I know I make mistakes in my work all the time, which is why I ensure it's read by several people and also edited thoroughly. Not only 'popular' novels suffer in this way – I've seen it in allegedly literary works, whose covers have been crowded with unctuous praise from 'names' and whose authors have even won awards for their writing.

It worries me that we are heading into literary Dark Ages, where standards plummet to the quality of text speak and the construction of language – our basic tool of communication – dissolves. Even now, (and perhaps for a long time), students emerge from schools and colleges barely able to string a sentence together. Friends of mine who are teachers and lecturers constantly lament the illiterate state of their students, many at so-called university level. The most horrifying part is that people at the top, with the power to do something about this situation, don't seem to care that much. Standards are lowered so that barely literate students can get degrees. I too see countless manuscripts from would-be writers that are almost unreadable, so poor is their grasp of the tools of their trade. And yet they think they have the ability to produce novels and stories, patently not realising they have to learn their trade – and most likely work hard to educate themselves in English language skills they were never taught at school – just like in any other profession. Perhaps this is a tide us old school writers cannot swim against and it's the inevitable fate of literature in our modern society, a heart-breaking dumbing down. I really hope I'm wrong.

Further Concerns About Modern Writing

Blog Post 8th March 2014

I've repeated certain ideas and personal niggles in this piece, which have appeared in earlier articles on writing in this section of the book. However, I think they're worth repeating.

I'm passionate about writing and care about the fate of new writers. In a recent blog, I wrote about the standard of writing I'm coming across nowadays, in terms of grammar, syntax, spelling and punctuation – essentially the tools of the trade. This generally refers to books I find self-published as E-books. But after reading a couple of recent *printed* short story anthologies, I'm driven to say that the poor standard of writing also extends to the actual story-telling. I'm not going to name names or point fingers, because that can simply start a needless war of words, but I do think the topic is worthy of discussion.

Primarily, I think the fault lies in the standard of editing that's now prevalent. There are still some remarkably good editors out there, but it seems to me some editors appear to see their job when compiling an anthology as simply checking the spelling and the worst of the grammatical woes, (and maybe only with Word's built in grammar and spelling checkers), but who don't offer comment on how a story might be strengthened or refined. Many new writers begin their careers by contributing short pieces to magazines and anthologies, which now also extends into e-publishing. And some of those new writers, while showing obvious promise and talent, need guidance to help hone their craft. I can remember working early in my career with editors like David Garnett, Ellen Datlow and David Pringle, (to name but a few who spring to mind – there were many), who would make great suggestions for how a story might be improved. Perhaps nowadays, in this age of entitlement, writers are less open to such invasive editing, even if they need it, so editors will therefore be less inclined to offer comment for fear of it being badly received or rejected. I myself have had authors withdraw stories from a collection because they weren't willing to make constructive changes. Strangely enough, the writers who are open to positive criticism are generally the most talented. It's as if they're hungry for ways to improve their work. Writers of poorer quality are usually the ones to have a tantrum if you offer any form of criticism. There are exceptions, of course, and some weaker writers crave learning, while some excellent writers are strict about not having a word of a piece changed. I'm just speaking generally.

What I fear most about the advent of e-publishing, and the fact that a lot more people have an avenue to get their stories into virtual print, is that they don't have the benefit of the apprenticeship that writers of the past enjoyed. Companies – and in some cases I refuse to call them publishers – have no care about nurturing a writer and helping them evolve. I don't blame the writers who I see publishing flawed work – they simply have a desire to write. The contract between writer and editor was always the hand of discipline, how to refine your work, tighten and improve it. I don't believe that some of the eBooks I see nowadays have had any of that applied to them. In one case, I saw an allegedly historical novel so full of wince-making anachronisms, it was almost unreadable. Even watching period TV shows would have given the author a basic idea of what and was not feasible in the time they chose to write about. Possibly one of the worst bloopers I read was of a new mother being welcomed home from hospital with banners and balloons by her in-laws. This was set in the 1920s. Did mothers even give birth in hospitals then? No way would in-laws have laid on the balloons and banners. It was cringe-making. Then, following on from that glaringly too-modern detail, it later followed that sleepless nights caused by the baby gave rise to a strain on the mother's marriage. She was presented as middle class. A woman of that class in that era would have had staff to deal with the child. The father would have been barely aware of it. People of that time wouldn't have had any idea of 'strains' on a marriage, especially caused by babies. They just made do, as was expected of them by their families and society. Those are just two examples of what was a book riddled with anachronisms. No research, no awareness of the era the author was writing about. And the publisher just accepted the manuscript and published it. That is no favour to the author. I wanted to read that book because the idea for it was great – a really good ghost story – but the ineptitude of the writing, and the lack of research, lost me about a third of the way through and I had to stop reading it. The ghosts were the most credible thing about it.

I really don't blame new authors for some of the appallingly weak novels and stories I've read recently. Many just have a gut-deep imperative to write, and in the past editors were the shepherds, who guided new writers to greater accomplishment. Nowadays, most new writers only have friends, or perhaps other fledgling writers, to rely upon for feedback and criticism. And in many cases they lack the guidance concerning the very basics of their craft – the words they use to conjure images in the minds of their readers.

All I can do is offer my own points for writers

Learn the tools of your trade.
Educate yourself concerning grammar, syntax, spelling and punctuation. There are many books out there to teach you. Once you know the rules, you have the authority to break them. And once you are proficient with your tools, a new world opens to you. You'll have far more control over your writing, and how to guide your readers through what you write, so they'll read every word as you intend for them to be read. Be clear. Be concise. Use your tools.

Let's look at examples. Grammar is *the* power. It sharpens prose and guides a reader to the meaning of your words. If your grammar is sloppy, your reader might need to re-read sentences to get the meaning, and in those moments, you've lost them. They're no longer immersed in the story, they're struggling for meaning. Verb forms are part of grammar, and the more active a verb the more exciting it is to your reader. Develop an ear for grammar. For instance, which sentence sounds more powerful to you? She is lying at my feet and is bleeding... or, She lies at my feet and bleeds? The more active form of the verb – the latter – is inevitably stronger. Put strength into your writing by using more active verbs. Avoid passive verbs as shown in the first example. Verbs are just a component of grammar; there is much more to it, of course. But it is fascinating to learn and once you see the results you'll be glad you learned it.

Syntax. This is the right words in the right order. Simple example: what's better? The cow jumped over the moon or over the moon the cow jumped? Both say the same thing but which is sharper, more meaningful? Syntax also involves seeing yourself as a camera, focusing in. What do people notice first? It's dark, it's cold, there are beetles beneath your feet. Mention the beetles first, then mention the cold and the dark, and your reader might have thought of any temperature and time of day when reading about the beetles. Focus. Use a film-maker's art. That is syntax.

Spelling. This part is simple. Just spell the words correctly and people can understand your writing better.

Punctuation. This is an art in itself. The different punctuation marks denote pauses, and you use these to guide the speed with which your readers read your prose. The longest pause is the full stop or period. A comma is a much shorter pause. Colons and semi-colons are in between. Dashes and brackets, and the suspenseful three dots (ellipses), are also used for speed-controlling the reader. There are rules about clauses, which need the embrace of commas, or the sharp report of a colon or semi-colon, that are more to do with grammar, but be aware you can put inflections on your words merely with deft punctuation.

Write about what you know

This gives you a voice of authority and makes your work credible. If you want to write about what you don't know – research. Meticulously. Give your work authenticity so that your reader is never jerked involuntarily out of the story by inaccuracy or something not credible. Detail is paramount. If you're writing about fantasy worlds, invest them with a level of detail and history so that readers feel they are stepping into a world that has existed for thousands of years. You don't have to slap this on with a trowel, but just subtle details here and there, and lore of the past. As an example, recently I wrote a supernatural story about certain aspects of the Catholic Church set in the 1950s. I found myself researching details every few paragraphs and changing the story because of anachronisms. These were just tiny details, such as who would have had a phone in those days (few), would a blue collar working man have eaten lunch in a pub (no), would a poor working-class family have had a fridge (again, no). Things we take for granted in our modern world can't be included in a historical, or often not even in a fantasy story, depending on the kind of world you're creating.

Read, read, read.

Analyse the books you like and figure out what works for you with them. Apply these rules to your own work. Also figure out what disappoints you, or what you don't like, and avoid that in your own writing.

Write from the heart.

If you love what you are writing, the chances are greater that others will love it too. If it's your first novel, write the book you've always wanted to read but have never found. But be aware you have to abide by points 1, 2 and 3.

Introductions

Dirty Work

Pat Cadigan
Mark V Ziezing, 1993

This book that you have picked up and (presumably) bought contains stories that are speculative fiction. I'd like to get that clear from the start. Although they will be enjoyed by lovers of science fiction, horror and fantasy, the stories are primarily Pat Cadigan speculating about the world she inhabits, and that is the world familiar to all of us; the same world that – occasionally – is unfamiliar to all of us too. Whether our belief system veers towards physics or something more mystical (is it possible to be more mystical than physics nowadays?), most of us, at some time, get a feeling that there just might be another side to reality that exists alongside our own. Perhaps more than simply one other side – perhaps a great tangle of them! In paranoid moments – or moments of solitude in the dark – you might think that maybe the conspiracy-freaks are right, and there really are weird people about, people who are unnervingly different to us, who could be hiding within our society. People with Another Kind of Knowing. Sometimes we might even get what appears to be glimpses of these people and their other, 'not our' worlds. You know those times. It's when coincidence aligns to alarming effect, invoking incredulity, bafflement and a creepy feeling up the spine. As an experiment, ask everyone you meet if they have ever experienced anything they have found inexplicable, strange, reality-challenging. I don't think I've ever met anyone who hasn't got their own weird story to tell. Pat Cadigan, undoubtedly, has a whole catalogue of them. She knows the other worlds of the Not-Quite-Normal quite intimately, I feel. She sees the secret people and accommodates them quite fearlessly within her stories. And yet, this is not to say her work can be placed solely in the realms of the fantastic, for what Pat writes about best, even in her most reality-shaping moments, is Life – our lives. She directs her clear sight into the viscera of estrangement, self-doubt, fear, political lunacy, loneliness and violence. Her hidden worlds and secret people are metaphors for all that is hidden and secret within us. The characters in Pat's stories are real people, never simply plot devices or ciphers; they just happen to be experiencing something quite bizarre for a little while.

My first experience of Pat's work was her debut novel, *Mindplayers*, which appeared in 1988. I'd already become acquainted with the cyberpunk novelists, and their offspring: *Mindplayers* had been heralded as another relative of this irreverent tribe. Now, while I had admired the neon extremities of cyberpunk, and post-cyberpunk, creations, marvelled at the slick-speak employed by the authors, the casual familiarity with mind-blowing technology, as a body of work it had never touched my emotions. Perhaps this was simply a characteristic of the genre. *Mindplayers* was to change my mind about that. After reading only a few pages, I knew I'd come across something different – and maybe, despite its trappings – it was. It wasn't just that the prose itself was a pleasure to read, (the rhythm of a novel is what tends to draw me into the story). Regardless of the sleek techno-trappings, *Mindplayers* transcended its supposed genre. It was about people; frail and vulnerable; tough and street-wise. The idiom Pat wielded was deft, yet there was a constant rhythmic rumble beneath the words that whispered of the cracking sanity of Deadpan Allie, the female protagonist (who makes a guest appearance in this collection). Disorientating mantras pervaded the text. Altered states of consciousness? Alerted snakes of consequence, of course. (A quote from the book.)

If *Mindplayers* was an outstanding achievement for a first novel, Pat's second book, *Synners*, had me in awe of her writing. The plot was convoluted, yet skimmed along with silvery ease. As in *Mindplayers*, the novel was permeated with mantras, little loops that stuck in the brain, the murmuring, insistent, almost sinister undercurrent that underlined the neuroses of certain protagonists within the story. Pat insisted to me she was not an aficionado of new technology, yet this was far from apparent in the book. However, the story was never sacrificed to the technology; the characters were (literally in some cases) part of it, yet vital and credible in their own right, with their own developed histories and futures. The sub-culture of the synners (hacker/punk/drug/music) was explored without resorting to cliché. Pat spoke with confidence and vision, almost as if she herself had experienced the wild life of her female lead, Gina. Also, Pat being a mistress of cynical asides, the book had been written with humour, even if it was often bitter sweet.

The stories in this anthology cover many themes, but one of their unifying factors is the twist in the tail, the final ironic flick of a sleek paw that, with careless, whimsical cruelty, toys with the reader. It might be you thought the story you'd been reading had finished, but no, she puts a last sentence down, just a few words, just a few slivers of something, well, sharp and glossy. Pat likes to let her readers run about between her claws, allowing them to believe they understand what's happening to them and will be allowed to escape, before she casually delivers the final blow she has been planning all along. Her stories never shrink from embracing every human feeling; sharp humour sits down with tragedy, the unexpected becomes manifest. The humour is often black, because of its devilish accuracy as it impales the human condition.

At first glance, 'New Life for Old' appears to be a light-hearted tale, a fairy story, but after lulling the reader into this false sense of familiarity, the story back-flips into a poignant stab at what it means to grow old, invoking the wistful inevitability of fading youth, the idyllic and best-remembered summer day that is all too short, the snapshot memory. The last line is devastating. I read this one aloud to a friend, starting off in a light-hearted voice, which gradually, involuntarily, changed in tone, to something distinctly more tremulous. At the end of it, hairs were standing up on my arms. My listener said one word: 'Brilliant!' And then, 'Are they all like that?'

Well, not exactly of course, because every story is different, but every one of them delivers. The stings in the tails vary in toxicity, but never fail to give a jolt, a rush, a feeling of 'Oh Yes!' Through her writing, Pat makes you feel as if you're being given insight into something arcane, and sometimes the complexities of her tale-weaving is like a juggler controlling a myriad flight of shining baubles. The intricacies of the plot, and the almost elusive concepts the author is exploring, are intertwined enough to perturb the brain, like when you attempt to get a grip on the infinity of Universe. I often think that when she's writing Pat must slip into some parallel level, whose rules and subtleties are almost beyond our ability to grasp. Yet in the end, mindful of her charges, the readers, she always leads us back to reality, aligns in our senses and our minds the threads of the story she is telling. 'Oh yes, of course! Alerted snakes of consequence, after all!'

The story 'Naming Names' also beguiles us at first into thinking we are in Recognisable Territory, through Pat's use of another motif from fairy-tale. Knowing a person's true and secret name allows the Knower to strip the Named of autonomy, to acquire a person's soul. This is a contemporary fantasy story, right, but our feet are firmly on the ground here, aren't they? Don't count on it! Gradually, surreality creeps through the familiar world. The protagonist's trip on the ferry, populated by secret people who move unseen among the passengers, where random snatches of conversation carried on the air apply directly to the protagonist's own life and needs, exemplifies perfectly Pat's silken use of language to convey the subtleties of her stories.

The story 'A Deal With God' – a loose sequel to 'Naming Names' – plays havoc with your senses of reality and time. Here, the language jumps through hoops at Pat's command, allowing her to convey her honeycomb of ideas without slipping or losing balance. It would be so easy to become lost in the plot, yet you emerge, perhaps a little dazed and disorientated, but aware you have experienced something *other*. Again. And you are breathless back in reality. Until the next time you pick up the book. Which is of course an impulse too strong to resist, even if the text can make you feel a little weird, a little unsure of whether real is real.

I feel strongly that these stories will resonate with their readers in different ways, according to the individual. They will get to you, all of you, (in both senses of the phrase), of that I am quite sure. When you put the book down, you will not come blinking back into daylight unmoved. There are secret messages, secret resonances, for everyone within the pages of this book. The stories work on more than one level, and the trip into their realities will differ for every one of you. The message of this introduction is: 'read these stories now.' Nothing more. In case you hadn't guessed.

Heaven Sent

Edited by Peter Crowther
Creed, 1994

Was it coincidence that the day the manuscript for *Heaven Sent* arrived on my doorstep, was also the day I met writer Andrew Collins for the first time? Well, it could have been, but for the subject matter of the manuscript and the current project of Mr Collins. Namely, angels. Both Andrew and Pete Crowther had contacted me because they knew of my interest in these winged beings, (of the leathery and feathery variety), and that I had written about them extensively in my own work. I have always been fascinated by angels – not the fluffy, twee denizens of cheap Christmas cards, but the darker, shadowy presences of occult literature and religious mythology, which I suspect prompted Pete to ask me to write an introduction to this collection.

Angel is a broad term, which covers an enticing selection of entities. In one of its most benign aspects, the angel is cast as an invisible guardian, a spirit guide, watching over its appointed charge in life and guiding the departing spirit into the unknown realm beyond death. Other legends speak of more aggressive protectors; monstrous creatures invoked in magical rites, (for good or ill), wielding various forms of occult weaponry: whirling, fiery swords, winds, vipers and thunderbolts. Elsewhere we find the holy avengers, culling damned souls, such as the seven Angels of Punishment, who include among their ranks such humourless entities as Kushiel, the 'Rigid One of God' and Makatiel, the 'Plague of God'. There is a brand of occultism devoted solely to invocation of angelic forms – Enochian Magic – which utilises the language of angels, said to have been transcribed by the Elizabethan occultist, John Dee. Angels are the intermediaries between the divine and the not-divine, messengers of the deity, dog's bodies of the heavenly spheres. They can bring Glad Tidings of Great Joy or point the Finger of Doom.

Andrew Collins is currently researching a book about the Nephilim, a breed of angel in which I've always had a deep interest and intend to write a novel about in the near future. The stories surrounding these sinister beings are ripe for plundering by writers, and synchronicity being what it is, there are no doubt at least a dozen authors working on synopses similar to my own at this very moment. According to lesser-known contemporaries of Old Testament books, the Nephilim were disreputable hybrids, spawned when a band of angels, known as the Watchers, went rogue, disobeyed heavenly law and took human women as lovers. The progeny of this union were monstrous babies, who had to be delivered by what amounts to Caesarean Section, and who grew up to be cannibalistic giants. Andrew has an encyclopaedia for a brain, (no, possibly an advanced supercomputer), and the stories, fables, and historical facts and fictions he can recall at lightning speed is phenomenal. I spent a day in his company attempting to absorb the torrent of information he had to impart, in the hope it would serve as a backbone for my proposed novel (in the event, I think I gleaned enough for at least a trilogy).

The fallen Watchers were dark and terrible; possessed of superior knowledge which they bestowed upon humanity against the ruling of their god, an act for which they suffered the most ghastly punishments, described in gleeful detail in the ancient *Book of Enoch*. It is doubtful these spirits would ever find employment posing for Christmas cards. Such was the intensity, the pervading atmosphere of dark power, surrounding these stories, that I was extremely nervous about turning the light off when I went to bed that night. For an agonising moment I thought I saw an unnaturally tall, shadowy form with glowing red eyes in the corner of my room, realising, after a heart-stopping moment, I was looking at the reflection of my clock-radio in the mirror. This would never do! Nightmares eagerly awaited me once consciousness was surrendered. On went the light; out came the manuscript to *Heaven Sent*. I hoped to find more benign spirits within its pages, and the first two stories I read that night mercifully calmed my nerves and, once I felt able to face the dark again, accompanied me into a demon-free slumber. (Fortunately, I had decided to read them in order, and I'm talking particularly to *you*, Ms Ptacek!)

I first began researching angelology in the (very) early stages of devising my Wraeththu trilogy around 1977. Luckily, I came across a very wonderful out-of-print book in the library where I worked: Gustav Davidson's *Dictionary of Angels*. Recently, the book has been reprinted, and I recommend it to anyone interested in angelology. Davidson's book is a must for every lover of trivia, stuffed as it is with a multitude of angelic lists, forgotten myths and infernal hierarchies, gleaned from a variety of religious traditions, including Judaism, Cabbala, Christianity, Islam and Zoroastrianism. I had never realised angels were so legion, literally, or so *specialised*. Not only are there several angels for each season, planet and weather condition, there are hundreds of others responsible for precise duties, such as Ram-Khvastra, the Angel of Rarefied Air; the Angels of Quaking (unnamed!); Zahun, the Angel of Scandal; Tubiel, the Angel Over Small Birds and Rahab, the Angel of Insolence. Naturally, there are angelic officers for the relatively common-place, exemplified by the Angels of War, Lust, Love, Death, Salvation, etc. For pregnant women, who have the time and the breath, there are seventy amulet angels which can be invoked at the time of childbirth, (reciting them may be one way to take your mind off the discomfort, I suppose). Many of the listed spirits seemed to be troublesome creatures, forever at odds with their presiding deity, and plotting to overthrow heavenly rule. The angels of ancient legend are rarely sugary creatures, adorned with only two big, feathery wings and garbed in white frocks. Originally, for example, the Cherubim were monstrous creatures. No adorable little babies with chubby faces and diminutive wings. One definition cites them as being a blue or golden yellow colour, having the form of a winged man but with a fourfold head: that of an eagle, lion, man and ox. They also stand on wheels and carry flaming swords. (See Garry Kilworth's story in this collection for a *Dictionairre Infernal* rendition of a cherub). Kerubiel, the leader of the Cherubim, is described as being 'full of burning coals'. The Seraphim, (another traditionally cute throng), are described as fiery serpents, having four faces and six wings, who roar like lions. Perhaps unfortunately, they are also fond of singing.

If you happen to be at the mercy of the demon of disease, Sphendonael, call for the assistance of the angel Sabrael – he's the only one who can help. Should you attempt to invoke Hauras, (once a celestial power, now fallen to bad times), make sure you don't do it in Hell, because he's a leopard there, and will only adopt a manlike shape when conjured up by an exorcist on Earth. Feeling uncontrollable jealousy? The angel Balthial will help you thwart the machinations of the evil genius responsible. Let's hope the angel Sebhael never sells his story to the tabloids; he's in charge of the books in which the good and evil actions of man (sic) are recorded. Should a love affair be going badly, a male can invoke the services of Miniel, who is able to 'induce love in an otherwise cold and reluctant maid; but for the best results, the invocant must be sure he is facing south'. Take heed. Oh, should you need a magic carpet, Miniel can oblige in that department, too. There is a patron angel for writers as well, although I've been unable to remember his name or look him up, which means, I think, he can't appreciate the way I'm describing his peers, and must be deliberately preventing me from misrepresenting him. Perhaps I should be careful. That's one guardian spirit I certainly don't want to lose as a friend!

But all the above are angels from the past. In this book, you will be reading about angels of the present, the newly-fledged denizens of the winged imaginations of their creators. The stories in this collection reflect what the term 'angel' means to each contributor. Several stories are concerned with the Guide into the Afterlife aspect, such as Charles de Lint's 'The Big Sky', with its dextrously-evoked shadow city, where the lost dead walk, shrinking from the Light, Christopher Evan's 'House Call', (having a distinctly sinister undertone), and with venomous humour in Jane M Lindskold's short, but acid-drop sweet, 'Relief'. Other stories tell of guardian angels, departed spirits, who return with messages for the living, such as Ken Wisman's 'Letting Go', which shows the dead can continue to learn from life, Kathy Ptacek's 'The Visit', where the ethereal vision of an angel reveals itself, at close quarters, to be something unpleasantly different to what it seems from a distance, Nina Kiriki Hoffman's 'Part Singing', where a living girl finds inspiration and courage from the dead, and Stephen Law's touching 'Gordy's A-Okay' (which even upon a second reading made me feel a bit lumpy-throated and misty-eyed). Other writers have totally reinvented the angel, such as Ian McDonald, in his story 'Steam', set on his personal wild and colourful terra-formed Mars, (featured in his novel *Desolation Road*), Judith Moffett in 'The Realms of Glory', with its mysterious denouement, (I'm still puzzling Judith: was it the real thing at the end or wasn't it?), and Ed Gorman in 'Synandra', where the Angel of Death takes on new flesh as she traverses time and space in her journey of destruction. If you want a real whiff of the inferno, put nose to page in John Brunner's exquisitely gruesome tale, 'Real Messengers'. In 'Spirit Guides', Kristine K Rusch's protagonist has a special relationship with the angels of destruction, but his enlightenment involves learning the exact nature of that relationship. In 'Wings', James Lovegrove takes us into an angel city, a post-modernist fable, where the heavenly hosts inhabit what seems to be a para-American town, and a young boy-angel learns how to cope with a crippling *difference* that has made him an outsider. Garry Kilworth, in 'Cherub', tells a cautionary tale of what can happen if you should invoke an angel in self-defence, and in Bruce D Arthur's 'Angel Blood', fallen angel takes on a distinctly alternative meaning. Gary Braunbeck's 'After the Elephant Ballet' is a surreal emotional journey (another misty, lumpiness when I read this, thanks Gary!), and the final story in the collection, the masterly 'In Gethsemane' by Stephen Gallagher, invokes the angel of conscience.

There is one other story, Michael Bishop's 'Spiritual Dysfunction', which I've left mentioning until last because the angels who manifest within it are probably the closest relations to those who rustle through the pages of Davidson's Dictionary. (The Angelspeak they use is certainly more tolerable than Enochian; I like to think angels have a sense of humour and a sharp turn of phrase!) The author draws upon one of my own favourite sections of Milton's Paradise Lost, concerning whether or not angels have sex, and if they do, how. The characters are 'real' angels in that Hashmal was traditionally the chief of the order of Hashmallim, the 'fire speaking angel', who 'surrounds the throne of God', Raphael is one of the archangels, and Sariela is (presumably) taken from Sariel, who was one of the fallen angels described in the books of Enoch, responsible for teaching humanity the forbidden knowledge of the 'courses of the moon'. As this could be interpreted as including a woman's monthly cycle, it's pertinent that Michael chose Sariel to be a female angel, for more than one reason. Angels, on the whole, are represented as male, although they are supposed to be sexless. There are very few instances of female angels in the old legends, which undoubtedly reflect the patriarchal views of when the stories were first created. Refreshingly, there are at least seven female angels in these stories, which show that the modern form is helping to redress the balance.

I have always found Pete Crowther to be a sympathetic and creative editor, with sensitivity for the feel of a story, and respect for the author's aspirations. The achievements of the individual writers aside, I'm sure he's been just as responsible for producing such a highly readable, thought-provoking and well-crafted collection. Don't just take my word for it. Read on. Mysteries await you, and journeys, and quite a few scares. But if by any chance one of the creepier offerings is the last one you read before turning off the light, just remember these stories are Heaven Sent.

And it's probably just your clock-radio you can see glowing in the corner.

Streaking

Brian Stableford
PS Publishing, 2006

I see Lady Luck slinking across the floor of a casino. She looks a lot like Kim Novak, in a blue satin strapless dress, 60s style, her blonde hair swept up in a chignon. I see her pausing behind the gamblers as they sit at the gaming tables. She's like one of the guardian angels from Wim Wenders' film, *Wings of Desire*. The gamblers can't see her, but perhaps they can feel her presence. Will she touch some of them on the shoulder tonight?

It's hardly surprising that humans have given Luck a semi-human face, and the totally human quality of capriciousness. Some people seem to have luck in abundance, while others are stalked by misfortune at every turn. Luck can stand by your side for years, then abandon you so thoroughly that it feels as if a trickster deity is in control and is now laughing at your fate, if not in your face. Is the distribution of good fortune random or preordained, and is there anything a person can do to improve their luck? Are some people just born with good luck in their genes?

In *Streaking*, Brian Stableford explores these questions from every angle. The protagonist, Canny Kilcannon, soon to be 32nd Earl of Credesdale, is a very lucky man. The 'streak' is the flashing visual effect he gets when his luck has touched the moment and somehow changed it. He's been told by his father their luck is an inherited trait that has to be nurtured and preserved, even appeased through ritual, but Canny isn't sure that's the answer. The truth behind his 'gift' might lie in New Physics, in Philosophy, Psychology or Mathematics, or even in the Occult. How much of the Kilcannon luck can be put down to coincidence, or simply being alert for omens and therefore finding them, and how much down to the esoteric workings of a genetic trait unmapped by human science?

I once heard a theory that each person has a finite amount of luck that is divided into sections, much like a pie. If, for example, you have a lot of luck in the romance area of your pie, then you might be lacking in the money, career, health or social life segments. In Chaos Magic, which is an occult discipline closely allied to quantum physics, it's believed you can change the distribution of the luck in your life. I actually think this is quite a dangerous idea, but intriguing nonetheless. Another face of Lady Luck is the Cosmic Joker, the Fool, and this is the form you work with to 'deconstruct the moment' as Brian refers to it. It's a psychological ritual, usually working with dice or some other random number/decision generator. You effectively put yourself into the hands of fate and for some time, perhaps a day, live by the dice, by random chance. It's said that by doing this you can force the moment, change reality, much as how Canny observes his luck working – although in the novel this is a spontaneous effect rather than a conscious action. However, the Fool is a fickle character and a trickster; he can take away as much as he as can give, and sometimes if you get what you desire, you might wish you hadn't. As one of the characters observes in *Streaking*, be careful what you ask for, because you might get it! And if you do force the moment, how much of reality will change? Is there not a risk that you'll lose some of the good along with the bad?

Another theory suggests that there is a finite amount of luck to go around the whole human race, (i.e. one enormous pie), and that if someone has a lot of it, then that means others will inevitably be lacking. And what if there is no such thing as luck at all, and the experiences of life are simply random, over which you can never have control?

Streaking winds through the maze of all these perplexing questions and theories, as Canny attempts to penetrate the mystery of his family's legendary good luck. His dying father has warned him to stay away from others who are similarly blessed, to ward against catastrophic effects, such as bringing down the terrible 'black lightning', the worst aspect of the streak. You can easily imagine that if these lucky people really existed, then the incidence of two or more of them competing in the same environment could spell disaster, and not just for them. Others might well be caught in the fallout as each strain of luck vies for dominance and control. In such a situation, it doesn't seem unfeasible that the black lightning could strike down to splinter reality.

In the hands of a lesser writer than Brian, the ideas might seem like utter fantasy, but one of the strengths of this tale is its plausibility. As you read, you can suspend your disbelief and really believe such things might and do happen. Brian has forty years of professional writing behind him, with an impressive array of novels, articles and non-fiction titles to his credit. *Streaking* is a mature and beautifully constructed novel, which invokes a sense of wonder in the literal sense.

Behind the story lie the misty realms of an imagined Utopia. It's no coincidence that the perfect village over which the Earls of Credesdale hold sway is named Cockayne, for the fabulous land of luxury and plenty. The people of Cockayne live in a kind of time capsule, as if enwombed against the harsh depredations of reality by the Kilcannon luck. The only inhabitants who suffer are those who have moved away from their roots. Canny obviously has a sense of obligation to those who live in his properties and work in the businesses that have come to replace the old mills, not least because they are as much beneficiaries of his family's gift as he is. His sense of responsibility wars with his desire for understanding, for experimentation, for – literally – pushing his luck. Upon attaining his title, he might have given up the gambling tables of the Riviera for a while, but his life is just about to get rather more... *interesting!*

There's little more to say without spoiling the story. Simply curl up somewhere comfortable and read the book. I suspect that if you took the time to interview a selection of 'professional' gamblers, they'd live more by superstition and omens than you might think. As you read, are there casinos somewhere, where the streak flashes above the tables, unseen except by the few? The dice fall, the roulette wheel spins, and Lady Luck haunts the air, waiting to dispense her favours. How lucky are you feeling today?

The Empty House and Other Ghost Stories/The Listener and Other Ghost Stories

Algernon Blackwood
Stark House Press, 2014

This introduction is prefaced by a blog post I wrote about the work, which I think it's relevant to include.

This week I've written an introduction for a new edition of Algernon Blackwood's first two short story collections, which will be combined into one volume by Greg Shepard – who some of you might remember published American editions of several of my novels, plus *The Oracle Lips* story collection, through his Stark House Press.

Blackwood is one of the most influential supernatural writers of the early twentieth century and inspired many other authors. I hesitate to use the term 'horror writer' for authors of his time, since to me the word horror nowadays often just entails blood, guts, torture, dismemberment, and so on, and I've never liked that kind of fiction. To me, the best horror is that which implies more than it shows; feelings of unease, the inexplicable, the subtly chilling. Anyway, I recommend Greg's book, which includes *The Empty House and Other Ghost Stories* and *The Listener and Other Stories*.

One thing I think is really important is that works like Blackwood's are still available for everyone. So many of the eBook editions you see of these 'historical' writers are really badly produced, full of errors, and in one case recently – utterly empty of everything except the first page. I've read quite a few of these eBooks, since I've been devouring stories of this kind recently, and have been astonished at the sloppy production, as if the text wasn't even read through once before it was slapped on the Kindle store. I know how difficult, if not impossible, it is to produce an absolutely pristine manuscript – mistakes will not be spotted because of human error – but really some eBooks have appalling amounts of them. Several stories have been virtually unreadable, owing to strange fonts and symbols littered all the way through. Hopefully, more publishers like Greg will restore these works with a bit of actual care.

Another thing I've noticed as I've been reading all these short story collections is how superior the older writing often is. It's noticeable particularly when an editor has collected the new with the old; so many of the new ones are weak, uninteresting, or just gore fests. Dull, in other words. Whereas there are some real gems to be found in the older writing, often by authors completely unknown, who perhaps just produced a few stories to be published in magazines of the time. There were a fair amount of women writers involved in the genre too, and I read one eBook *The Lady Chillers: Classic Ghost and Horror Stories by Women Writers*, which was excellent. All of the collections have a few duds in them – inevitably – but this one was superior to most. Sadly, you won't find collections by the majority of these writers, although there is a printed version of Edith Wharton's ghost stories available. The eBook of Edith Nesbit's ghost stories – forget it. This was the one I bought that was an empty file. (Actually it looks as if since I complained to Amazon it's been removed from the Kindle store.) The Mary E Wilkins Freeman Megapack eBook is worth getting, despite the second half of the book comprising rather twee children's stories. The first half, the supernatural tales, is great.

The Introduction

I love tales of the supernatural, the weird and the unexplained. This love began in childhood and has never lessened, and even now – to me – the masters and mistresses of the spooky story are those who popularized the genre in the nineteenth and early twentieth centuries. Modern horror often tends to rely upon gore and extreme violence, inspiring voyeuristic glee, (or plain disgust, depending on the reader/viewer), rather than the delicious chills conjured by the best ghostly tales of earlier decades. The impression of some unearthly creature creeping towards me on hands and knees in the dark is more genuinely horrifying than any visceral image of dismemberment or torture, which leaves little to the imagination and just makes me turn away, nauseated.

This book celebrates the work of Algernon Henry Blackwood, (1869–1951), who was one of the most influential supernatural writers of his time. The stories in this volume include those that were originally published in *The Empty House and Other Ghost Stories* (1906) and *The Listeners and Other Stories* (1907) – Blackwood's first two published collections.

Born in Kent, England, Blackwood travelled widely in his life, spending some years working as journalist (among other jobs) in New York. This is why he never suffers from that fault found often in writers who try to set their stories in both America and the British Isles. Often, their native tongue – and misconceptions about the 'other' country – interferes with the authenticity of the tale. A native New Yorker can spot a story written by someone who's never been there, never mind lived there, and the same goes for a Londoner reading an 'English' tale written by an American who's never set foot on British soil. Blackwood could slip confidently into the atmosphere and patois found on both sides of the Atlantic.

Algernon Blackwood inspired many other writers of 'the weird', among them H. P. Lovecraft and William Hope Hodgson, and more recently Ramsey Campbell. He wrote prolifically, publishing a large number of novels and short stories, as well as plays, most of which can be categorised as 'weird', although he also dabbled in romances and war stories.

Perhaps what makes Blackwood's work so *realistic*, if I may use that term for stories of this genre, is that he was able to draw upon his own experiences, and not just those of travel. He was fascinated by the occult and the supernatural, and was a member of several societies and organisations associated with them. As a member of one of the factions of the famous, if not infamous, Hermetic Order of the Golden Dawn, (along with other writers such as Arthur Machen and W. B Yeats), he could write with authority about the Qabala and other magical subjects. He also joined The Ghost Club and The Psychical Research Society – enabling him to investigate allegedly haunted houses. Many of his stories are clearly based upon such events, even if Blackwood embellished them to be more ghostly and scary – as any creative writer would!

One character recurs in *The Empty House and Other Ghost Stories*, the psychic investigator Jim Shorthouse, who sometimes seems to be thrown haplessly into investigations rather than through an organised plan. In 'The Empty House', Jim is persuaded by his doughty Aunt Julia to spend the night in a building known to be haunted.

"…and it is the aroma of evil deeds committed under a particular roof, long after the actual doers have passed away, that makes the gooseflesh come and the hair rise. Something of the original passion of the evil-doer, and of the horror felt by his victim, enters the heart of the innocent watcher, and he becomes suddenly conscious of tingling nerves, creeping skin, and a chilling of the blood. He is terror-stricken without apparent cause."

Needless to say, Jim and Aunt Julia *do* experience the supernatural echoes of a past murder in the house, and end up leaving the place – scared almost senseless – far sooner than they'd planned. While there are deliciously frightening images in the story, there's also a light touch of humour in the relationship between Jim and Julia. Perhaps there was a female character similar to Aunt Julia in Blackwood's own life, who established his interest in the supernatural and investigating the paranormal. I like to think so.

The hauntings in this collection are varied. In 'A Case of Eavesdropping', the protagonist, living in a boarding-house, is annoyed by loud arguments late at night in the room next to his. When driven to complain and investigate, he discovers an empty room, but the tale does not end there…

In 'Keeping His Promise' a somewhat lazy student, attempting to catch up on neglected studies, is visited in the middle of the night by a friend he's not seen for years, a friend who behaves most strangely, and who disappears, leaving behind him only a snore... that persists.

'The Woman's Ghost Story' could be called a romance, in which the protagonist overcomes her terror of the supernatural to redeem a lost soul.

There are different kinds of ghost to discover in this combined collection, as well as other enigmas.

Blackwood's love of nature and the mystery of the natural world shines from much of his work. He adored the 'great outdoors' and was reputed to be rather a loner, a mystic, more at home mountain-climbing than attending literary parties. One of his stories in particular, 'May Day Eve', not only illustrates his love affair with the unseen – the essential *goddess* of the land – but conjures its inexorable power and how humans are but ants upon it. The protagonist, a doctor, is on his way to his friend's house, a folklorist, whose beliefs in the supernatural the doctor scorns and finds ludicrous. As he journeys across a wild landscape on foot, his sureness in mundane reality is seriously challenged and eventually crumbles. In particular, one paragraph made my skin tingle:

"Then as I lay gazing dreamily into this still pool of shadows at my feet, something rose up, something sheet-like, vast, imponderable, off the whole surface of the mapped-out country, moved with incredible swiftness down the valley, and in a single instant climbed the hill where I lay and swept by me, yet without hurry, and in a sense without speed. Veils in this way rose one after another, filling the cups between the hills, shrouding alike fields, village, and hillside as they passed and settled down somewhere into the gloom behind me over the ridge or slipped off like vapor into the sky."

This natural force is not depicted – in any part of the story, which does become weirder – as brutal or malevolent, but simply impartial and massive. Whether the same can be said for the forces Blackwood's protagonists find themselves confronting in 'The Willows', (again, one of my favourites), is another matter.

This story involves a canoe journey by two men along The Danube, and how they have to camp for a couple of days upon an eerie island while the elements rage around them, making further progress by water impossible. The river, the wind, even the willow trees that crowd the island, eventually combine into a physical threat, but incomprehensible, uncanny and beyond human explanation. What is clear is that no matter how great their need for shelter, whatever lives on that island is inimical to the travellers and cannot be bargained with.

"With this multitude of willows, however, it was something far different I felt. Some essence emanated from them that besieged the heart. A sense of awe awakened, true, but of awe touched somewhere by a vague terror. Their serried ranks, growing everywhere darker about me as the shadows deepened, moving furiously yet softly in the wind, woke in me the curious and unwelcome suggestion that we had trespassed here upon the borders of an alien world, a world where we were intruders, a world where we were not wanted nor invited to remain – where we ran grave risks perhaps!"

He was right, of course, but even from that first investigation of the island, prodded subtly by the paranormal, the protagonist had no idea what was in store for him and his friend.

You can tell from reading this story that while Blackwood might not actually have encountered an island on The Danube occupied by non-human yet sentient *beings,* he must have made a similar journey, because he writes with such authority and detail. He must at some time have experienced the power of the elements and, perhaps, huddled in a tent, fearful he might not survive the storm, with the willow trees rattling, the wind making voices in their whipping branches; his imagination peopled that place with ancient spirits, against whom the logic of science and cool intellect are powerless.

Not all of the stories are supernatural in the literal sense. For example, in 'Max Hensig – Bacteriologist and Murderer', in which Blackwood clearly writes fondly of his time as a journalist in New York, a reporter is sent to interview a prisoner accused of killing his wife. Finding the man utterly unnerving, and having no doubts at all about his guilt, the reporter implies as such in his subsequent article, only to incur the wrath of Hensig, who is acquitted. This is a story of fear, paranoia and revenge, and includes the rather unusual theory of a person being able to reach a certain point of clarity while completely drunk, in which they are able to act in an almost superhuman manner.

'The Insanity of Jones' investigates reincarnation, and a debt between souls. Jones works in an office, the kind of job that is hell on earth in its spirit-throttling dullness. But strangeness creeps into Jones' life in the form of a man he feels he once knew, but not in this life. His boss, he is certain, is evil and has to be punished for crimes in a former existence. Insanity indeed… or perhaps unfinished business. This story is more gory than any of the others in this collection, but not gratuitously so. The violence, in this case, is essential to the tale.

The stories in this collection, just a few of which I've talked about here, can be revisited to discover new nuances and insights. The first time, you might read them just for the thrill but subsequent readings allow you to bask in Blackwood's skill as a writer, and also his ideas. A thoughtful, spiritual man – who happily for us could also tell a rattling good yarn!

Legenda Maris

Tanith Lee
Immanion Press, 2015

Legenda Maris is the first of a series of themed short story collections that Tanith Lee planned to publish through Immanion Press. Tanith died on 24th May 2015 at the age of 67. We see the publication of this book as our tribute to a remarkable author with whom we were privileged to work for several years and whose writing I personally have adored and found inspiring since I began reading it back in the 70s. While some of these stories have been in print before, Tanith always ensured that any new collection of her work included unpublished pieces. The new tales in this book were written only a few months ago, and are among the last ones she wrote. By collecting her stories within a theme, Tanith produced a new work entirely – almost like a series of chapters in a novel where the characters of each chapter never meet. In this work particularly, the only recurring protagonist is the sea. And the sound of it, the smell of it, permeates every story.

As most people who are familiar with Tanith's work will know, to say she was a prolific writer is an understatement. She lived and breathed writing, and even when incapacitated by illness endeavoured to keep working. She was reading the proofs of this book and marking corrections on them only a week or so before she died. Producing words almost continually never meant a lessening of standards. Tanith's stories were – and are – always fresh and innovative. She had an ability to conjure atmosphere in a way that only the best writers can. To read her work is to immerse yourself in her dreams and visions. She accomplished what many aspire to: virtual realities, magical worlds, in which you simply forget you are reading. You are there.

Tanith described her writing as 'channelling'. Stories poured out of her, characters spoke through her. While for some authors, writing can be like a war with their ability to describe accurately what they see so vividly in their minds, for Tanith writing was never a struggle. This was a wonderful gift, almost an extra sense. It speaks to me of a serene confidence; she never doubted for a moment that she was a story-teller to her very core – it was her *purpose* – and the buffets and blows of the publishing industry, which quite frankly was not always good to her, never undermined that confidence nor damaged her creativity.

The new stories in this book, 'Leviathan' and 'Land's Edge, The Edge Of The Sea', were written when Tanith was aware she didn't have much time left in this life, and this makes them particularly poignant. They explore passing and change, but also eternity and cycles, the *sureness* of life, as well as its ebb and flow. They are written with dignity and strength. With Tanith's passing, the world has lost a great writer, but many of us have also lost a beloved friend. The words of some of these friends can be found at the beginning of this book.

The less recent stories in *'Legenda Maris'* include a couple of my favourite Tanith tales 'Magritte's Secret Agent' and 'Because Our Skins Are Finer'; like strange dreams washed up on the shore of sleep, they stay with you long after you've finished reading. Several of the other pieces are uncollected, and I'd not even read them myself before Tanith sent me the manuscript for the book. These had been published previously in magazines or anthologies, so I suspect they will be new to many other readers of this collection too. The cover was created from an original collage by Tanith, which I scanned into the computer in two parts, (it was a long picture!), and which Immanion artist Danielle Lainton then 'stitched' together deftly so you cannot see the joins. Tanith's husband, John Kaiine, then worked on the picture some more to create the beautiful finished image that now adorns this book.

John wishes Tanith's work to continue, and part of this will be to go forward with the collections she planned to publish through Immanion Press. For now, though, please enjoy this jewel-spilling treasure chest of tales. And listen to the sea.

On Myth, Magic and Healing

The Everness Kiss:
Courting the Vampyre
1988, revised 1993

The following piece was originally commissioned by Darren Bentley, for his fanzine, Dreams from Within, (now defunct) in 1988. I rewrote it extensively, and it appeared in another fanzine, Twisted Souls in 1993.

LISTEN...

...And then he came forward into the yellow candlelight.

No shadow across my bed, no fetid breath of grave stink. Just this: lean and bleached as a salt-scoured bone; tall too, almost as if the whiteness of him was but a shadow, and stretched...

His eyes were of that burning blackness associated with Lilith's tribe, his lips red and swollen with the living juice of our knowledge-tree, but oh, there was beauty there. His hair was the black crow's wing, filled with scent of the elemental currents.

And his hands, sculpted with an artist's care, would stroke music from my flesh. I wanted, to infinity, his arms, his flesh, his Fatal Kiss...

I fancy that in these unbenighted times, there are poor pickings for the lust-lorn, seeking that most dark of seductive oblivions, the Vampyre Embrace. We live in a world of info-technology, eco-powders and fast-food convenience. The flesh and the spirit, once holy temples, are now parking lots. Sex, most potent of ancient magicks, has become sanitised and de-sanctified, and if that's not bad enough, it can now be a positively lethal practice. A suspect and shorn siren, sex has been undressed, dissected, and laid out on the surgeon's slab of popular media, pornography, and medical information posters for all to examine. (A lot of people even dress to look like occupied condoms nowadays. Can anyone in a shell suit really be considered an object of desire?) Regarding matters spiritual, our most hidden traditions have been de-mystified and commercialised, repackaged in bright new colours (safe for children) and marketed under the brand name 'New Age'. Where the eye of bat in these deliberations? The power of Woman de-clawed, unfanged.

So, the darkest, most secret corners of life have been violated; excavated and dragged into the mundane. Crumbling castles (English Heritage: oak leaf badge) have been theme-parked into family Sunday afternoon tourist retreats, their ghosts contained or exorcised by so much humdrum mediocrity. Haunted forests (with plaque to proclaim them as such) are veined with well-beaten paths. If something glitters through the rustling shadows, it is only the discarded, crumpled husk of a Coke can. The eyes of darkness are blinded and streaming, caught in the headlight glare of soulless civilisation. Cities and wilderness alike are acrawl with the unchecked bacteria growth of burgeoning humanity. Vampyres have no hiding place today. Have they?

For some, idolatry of the vampyre is the ultimate sado-masochistic fantasy: submission unto death. A fanciful form of nihilism, which is neither productive nor creative, but merely a fashion accessory. The vampire legends are romantic, inspired by our needs: longing, love, desire, lust and power. But they are so easily devalued.

The traditional concept of the vampyre - the repulsive ghoul of less than bedworthy countenance - has evolved into the rampant incubus/succubus of screen and printed page. The dribbling, skeletal fiend is obsolete, its niche swept out, tastefully lit by candles in elaborately-worked receptacles, and now occupied by the debonair wo/man in black who, with polished fang, is always beautiful, always irresistible, invariably deadly, but winsomely vulnerable too.

As humans, faced with this fantastic, endangered species of shrinking, limpid undead, we can be the protectors who shield them from the harmful spore of UV (although we need to protect ourselves from that nowadays). Defenders of the enigmatic predators, no garlic cloves will sully our pantry shelves. To entice the minions of the shattered dark to our thresholds, we might leave a saucer of blood at the back door, awaiting the dark or the full of the moon. Ah, but one should not poke fun at serious gods. And gods the vampyres are: our bat-winged philanderers of the twilight. The world is badly scoured of mystery; shadows dispelled by the light of science and technology, or so 'They' would have us believe. But we know better, don't we? As fleshless gods and top-heavy religions disintegrate and perish in a rotting morass of outmoded dogmas, we ourselves become the Creators of potent new mythologies. Why? Because we need to. The sultry swish of satin whispers along the damp, night-time streets of sulphur-lit suburbia. The vampyres prowl.

Vampyres are BIG business nowadays. As Stoker's original (anti)hero is brought to luscious, mysterious life upon the exalted silver screen, (the new god in all his terrifying, breath-taking, mysterious seductiveness - props and sets to match), embodying the ultimate in quick-byte sustenance, so vampyre novels, good, and not so good, continue to rustle their way onto book shop shelves – a longer, more abiding feast. I even wrote a vampyre novel myself, though sadly saw it published a year before the film hype (I'm an artist, yes, but the mis-timing still galls a little). In *Burying the Shadow* (Headline, 1992), I essayed to fulfil the vampyre-lover's most satyric dream; the sup, the commerce between immortal and mortal, was mutually sustaining; the staff of life in return for art, for knowledge. This was a metaphor for the true function of the vampyre in our personal mythologies: in return for blood, they give us beauty, they give us something beyond the mundane world, a glimpse into the star-sequinned dark, where anything is possible and life is not finite, nor rimed with trivia.

The real world is often such a bore. How can anyone be blamed, then, for desiring the smouldering glance of dark, hooded eyes in dim light, a luxury of caressing hair across the trembling victim's face, firm yet feverish lips upon the neck, the sting, the sting, etc., etc.? The werewolf, ghost and man-made monster, as sex idols, simply do not compare. The vampyre is pan-sexual, beyond gender division, an icon of desire. We don't know, can't really guess, what it feels like to be sucked to death, but we can bet our eyes it's an incredible rush. Vicariously, we spectate as screen surrogates die and suck, again and again, in a foaming wave of glorious red. And there have been memorable examples of the genre; the Vogue-style, soft-focus eroticism of *The Hunger*; the camp, meanderingly-plotted, yet visually-appealing *Vampires of Venice* and its more compact pre-cursor, *Nosferatu*; the street realism of *Near Dark* – vampyres among us – and the fast-paced, not-wildly-credible-but-entertaining-all-the-same carousel of *The Lost Boys*, culminating more recently in the lush extravagances of *Bram Stoker's Dracula*, the Oldman, Rider, et al vehicle.

And if we are not spectating, the ichor can be tasted through the pages of novels, such as those by Anne Rice, Tanith Lee and Brian Stableford.

....She always sits alone. Glass upon the table; finger tracing its rim, around and around. Long, red, red nails. She is smiling at the glass. Feels me staring. Tosses up her head, tosses back her hair. How white her skin; her eyes are full of mordant laughter. She puts her elbow on the table, rests her chin on her hand and smiles at me. Taps, with one lacquered talon, her sharp, white teeth...

Men would die for such an invitation.

Bound up in our cultural taboos, the vampyre kiss can be seen not only as a metaphor (extended) for simple osculation (when we kiss, are we not, in truth, desiring to eat our lover?), but for oral sex as well: sinking to oblivion, experiencing the ultimate in altered states, as the suckee floats in the beatific condition of hyper-consciousness. Of course, those interested in achieving such elevated heights don't need a predatory, supernatural immortal to achieve them. But that's another story. Racially/ unconsciously, humanity grabs in the dark at half-seen realities. Sometimes they guess right, is all. Perhaps it's part of human programming that the metaphor has to be created, so that the individual can handle the concept.

So, we dream up our demonangels, dredge them up from the dark, make them live. They have their hiding places after all; our minds. We send them out onto the streets and hope they find their way back to us. We'll be waiting, scared of the night, hiding under the bed-covers, for the rustle in the corner of the room, the sigh of breath, the scent of cold air and musk. One night, when we peek over the blankets, there might be more than moonlight in the room with us.

Maybe.

Bast and Sekhmet: Eyes of Ra

Article for *Monas Hieroglyphica* Magazine
February 1999

People have asked me why Eloise Coquio (my co-author) and I wanted to write *Bast and Sekhmet: Eyes of Ra*, a non-fiction book on Egyptian goddesses, specifically Bast and Sekhmet.

The reasons were threefold. Firstly, we'd come across so much interesting material in our magical work we wanted to share it. Secondly, there are too many New Age and witchcraft books on the subject of Egyptian gods and magic that bear little resemblance to reality, and have reinterpreted the past to fit it into the Western Tradition scheme of things. We felt we should redress the balance and present a well-researched view of ancient practices. Thirdly, there has not yet been a book devoted solely to occult work revolving around Bast and Sekhmet. We know that a huge amount of people are drawn to these goddesses, but in order to know more about them, you have to glean lots of little bits of information from many different sources. While we do think that a bit of hard work and research is good for any practising occultist, some of these texts are very difficult to acquire and you have to wade through a lot of material you don't want, in order to find the things you do. In *Bast and Sekhmet*, we wanted to present the information in a clear, unified form. There is undoubtedly much more to discover, but at least our book gives people a starting point, and most importantly dispels a lot of the fluffy, newly-invented myths about the goddesses.

In recent times, and especially so in America, reinterpretations of Bast and Sekhmet have arisen, which in our opinion are not only intrinsically 'wrong' but also do these ancient goddesses a discourtesy. Sekhmet is not a nurturing mother goddess, nor a sex kitten. Her colour ray is red, and she represents a very strong, fiery energy. In Cabbalistic terms, she belongs in Geburah. She has warlike aspects, and was known as a bringer of plagues, although, strangely enough to our modern perceptions, she was also regarded as a healer, and her priesthood were usually physicians. For us, Sekhmet brings courage, strength and energy, and we approach her when we feel a lack of these things in our lives. We have also petitioned her for help with legal problems, serious illness and matters of personal protection. We do not feel we can approach her unless we have a dire need. To us she is the spiritual equivalent of the 'big guns'.

Bast, on the other hand, has a more amiable aspect. Although, in ancient times she was very similar to Sekhmet, in that she was regarded as an Eye of Ra, and therefore an instrument of the sun's power to smite the enemies of the pharaoh, she eventually evolved into a more gentle form. There's no doubt that Greek influence in the later stages of Egyptian history played a great part in this transformation. Unlike Sekhmet, Bast does have connections with motherhood, so she can be seen as more of a mother goddess. However, we feel strongly that this is something entirely different from the modern concept of the mother goddess. Bast is still a cat, and as likely to claw as purr. Cats are protective of their kittens, and in this regard Bast makes a good mother, but she is no benevolent earth goddess. She is sometimes now perceived as a moon goddess, which is not entirely accurate if you want to stick to the original Egyptian conception of her, which made her entirely solar. However, the Greeks equated Bast with their own goddess Artemis, who certainly was a lunar deity. Therefore, Bast acquired this aspect, and as it has been in place now for a couple of thousand years, we think it has to be seen as valid, even if it deviates from Bast's original form. If we look at the Cabbala again, even if Bast was once at home solely in Geburah, she now has Netzach qualities, and perhaps because of the moon aspect, Yesod.

We asked for contributions from people who work magically or spiritually with Bast and Sekhmet, so that in one chapter of the book we could show how people interact with these goddess forms now. The results were very interesting and showed incredibly different perspectives. Some people were heavily into Egyptian beliefs as an organised religion and explained how they try to remain faithful to the original practices. Others came from a distinctly more magical background, where the faith aspect did not take centre stage. The examples we give in the book only give a brief glimpse into the vast array of differing beliefs and views that are out there. We did a lot of research on the Internet and were astonished to discover how many web sites were devoted to Bast and Sekhmet, as well as many other Egyptian gods. It was literally thousands, too many to look through.

We have a temple group that concentrates on the Bast and Sekhmet material, but we are not religious about this. We also celebrate the eight seasonal festivals from a Celtic perspective, and perform workings centring on other gods and goddesses when they are pertinent to the work in hand. Because so little information remains about the feline goddesses, we do a lot of visionary work, in which we attempt to project our minds back into the past in order to obtain knowledge. Of course, this has to be seen as entirely subjective, and little of what we see and experience can later be verified as fact, because the source material no longer exists, but it has helped us shape our magical system and create vivid rituals. We've had some intriguing results from visualisations on the goddess Tefnut, who also had a leonine-headed form. All of our workings involve a certain amount of visualisation or path-working, which we have found to be very effective.

Bast and Sekhmet: Eyes of Ra is published by Robert Hale.

A Life of Magic

Web Site Article, 1999

I have never made any secret of the fact that I am what most people would term an occultist. My interest in all things magical began at an early age, and in order to answer some of the questions I receive from readers, I'd like to talk about how this came about and how it has since influenced my work.

Even as a child, I was interested in ghosts, the supernatural and ancient legends. I was fascinated by the myths of Egypt, Crete and Greece, and was encouraged to read about them by my parents. As a teenager, I became aware of the life-force, without knowing what it was. I sensed that it was possible to shape reality, to impose my will upon it to effect change. I knew nothing about witchcraft, and indeed shared the majority's uninformed view that it was probably dangerous, if not evil.

By the time I was nineteen or so, I'd got in Tarot, and was surprised about how accurate it could be. Even now, I have a strong sceptical streak, but I do think it's healthy to maintain that, otherwise you can go skipping off to the land of the fairies and never return! I started to read books on magic, and was particularly impressed by the work of Marian Green. Reading her *Magic for the Aquarian Age* taught me about the energy I'd sensed in the world around me. I still shied away from any organised form of magic, and never considered joining a group of any kind. My magic was personal to me.

Then, in my twenties, a friend of mine, who shared my interests, suggested that we form a study group, in which people who were adept at different divining skills could pool their resources and learn from each other. My friend placed an advert in the local press. My forte was still Tarot, whereas my friend was heavily into dream analysis, but we soon attracted others, who were into astrology, runes, colour psychology and the like. We used to meet on a Sunday afternoon and for the first time I realised it was actually very enjoyable to share my occult interests.

After some weeks a new member joined the group, who was far older than the rest of us. He listened quietly to what we all had to say for a while and then told us he was a third degree Wiccan priest, and his interest lay in that direction, although he was not actively working with a coven at the time. At first, we were all very wary of this, and I must admit I felt uncomfortable with this newcomer's subtle approach to us, as if he was searching for recruits. I've always been very suspicious of that kind of thing, whatever religion is involved. However, he recommended some books to us to read and after meeting with him a few times, we realised he was not some kind of manipulative ogre, but just an elderly man who had a lot of experience and a strong and passionate belief in white magic. He was lonely and partly disabled, and clearly looking for people to work with. He felt that we were merely scratching the surface with our delvings into divination. If we were really interested in the subject, we should learn what magic was all about. I read Doreen Valiente's books and the work of Janet and Stewart Farrar, as well as many other magical titles. There were still aspects of Wicca that I didn't like – particularly the working naked part and certain components of the initiation ceremonies that smacked of bondage and S&M to me. But our new friend told us we did not have to get our kit off if we didn't want to.

To cut a long story short, we were introduced to a woman who ran a magical group in a nearby town. She agreed to teach us, with a view to initiating us eventually into Wicca. From her, we learned about meditation and other magical techniques. We were invited to attend one of her group's seasonal festivals, held in the open air, and I think this experience was what really fired my interest. I had never participated in anything like it before. It moved me to tears. The ceremony, the charges and the ritual actions were like poetry and drama, but with a strong spiritual undercurrent that seemed to touch me physically. I loved the sense of unity between group members, the feeling of connection with the divine in nature, and, it has to be said, the knowledge that I was involved in something that many people, through their own misunderstanding, thought was dark, dangerous and frightening.

Unfortunately, the glow eventually dimmed. I realised that the hierarchical nature of Wicca was not for me, and that the people involved were only human and not the great gurus I'd wanted them to be. I left the group before I was initiated, and with some friends decided to form my own group, which would be non-hierarchical and a departure from Gardnerian witchcraft, with its tier of initiations and set rituals. I felt that if magic was the search for self-knowledge, it could not be force-fed, and no-one could assume control of others to impart that knowledge. This was the product mainly of my inherent loathing of authority. I wanted to be part of a democratic group, where we learned from each other, and took it in turns to lead important rituals. With hindsight, I can see that my youthful zeal was blind to the fact that we all need guidance from more experienced practitioners, but I was still smarting from the conflicts I'd experienced in the Wiccan group and wanted to turn my back completely on any kind of dogma. The fundamental principles of Wicca, appreciation of the earth, nature and the honouring of an earth goddess and her consort, still appealed to me, but I felt there was something missing. I could never recapture the feeling I'd had during that first outdoor ritual.

My friends and I wrote many rituals, which we performed together. We experimented with various techniques, and our ceremonies became ever more complicated and elaborate. Eventually, one of the founder members thought we were losing sight of what we should be doing. We had become indoor dramatists, when really we should have been out in a field somewhere, just experiencing the raw energy of nature. At the time, I hotly refuted this, but now I can see my friend had hit on a certain truth. Neither of us were completely right, but we were too inexperienced to realise we needed to find a balance between the two views.

My friend left the group, and for a couple of years the rest of us continued on, until people drifted away one by one, as they moved house, acquired new partners or had children. After the last person had been swallowed by the maternity wing, I decided not to try and form a new group. The politics and dynamics of group working were too exhausting and I'd never found that idyllic state of co-operation, tolerance, consideration and openness I'd been seeking. It was undoubtedly better to work alone. What I hadn't considered was that I was partly responsible for not being in the kind of group I wanted. I still had a lot to learn.

Some years later, I was having a late night chat with a close friend, and we touched upon the subject of magic. She asked me to tell her my experiences, which I did. Then, somehow – and I still can't remember how it came about – one of us suggested we should do something together. We decided we'd keep this completely private and not even tell our partners or other close friends. We were not looking to form a group, but to experience spirituality for ourselves. The first ritual we did together, which was a seasonal festival, was exciting and joyous. We performed it on a night when we knew my partner would be going out, and waited until he'd left the house before we prepared a room and ourselves for the rite to come. I was envious of the deep fulfilling feelings my friend experienced that night and saw that they mirrored what I'd felt myself all those years ago in that first Wiccan ritual. It made me realise that the first ever magical working is a bit like losing your virginity. It can never be the same again, because once you've done it, it becomes partly demystified. Still, we went on to do many more workings, and those nights for us were very special. It was only when my partner found out what we were doing that the trouble started.

It wasn't that he didn't like it or disapproved, but he wanted to get involved himself. Inevitably, my friend's partner was told of our activities, and he too, having a great interest in shamanic magic, wanted to take part. Why couldn't they? What did we do that we didn't want them to see? Well, nothing, apart from the fact that those nights had been completely ours. The secrecy had intensified our spiritual experience. Eventually, we gave in, just because it was easier, and before we realised it, we had a group. Other people joined us, and although the group was never formal, friends of like mind would just come along to various festivals or specific workings and take part. My best friend was affected more strongly by this than I was. I was used to working in a group, and in fact quite enjoyed this new one, where because it was informal, we didn't encounter the same problems I'd experienced before. But my friend missed the way we'd worked before, just the two of us. She felt that having men present changed the atmosphere, and although this wasn't bad in itself, the simple difference didn't suit her.

Our magic was never about religion, worshipping individual gods and goddesses. We did it to connect with the universal energy and to further our self-evolution. After we'd been working like this for some time, I met Andy Collins and Debbie Benstead, and this opened up a whole new world for our group. Andy and Deb taught us all a different way of doing things, something they called 'results magic'. They never concentrated solely on the concept of the 'lord' and 'lady' in terms of god-forms. Through their research for Andy's books, they had a vast knowledge of the deities of the world. If they wanted to perform a ritual to achieve a specific result, they would focus the working on a god, goddess, angel or spirit that was most pertinent to the circumstances. Through them, we experienced rituals of many different belief systems. The energy for each one felt different, and it made me realise that all gods are just masks for different frequencies of the universal life-force.

For each of the seasonal festivals, Deb had written a ritual that did not resemble anything I'd done before. There was no circle casting, no purification of salt and water, not even a summoning of the quarters. To begin a ritual, she would construct a visualised 'cone of power' in which to work, and the main ritual itself revolved mainly around visualisation, with certain symbolic actions that each participant had to do, relevant to the character of the festival. For Imbolc, Deb wrote a ritual focusing on the goddess Brigid, for spring equinox, it was Ellen, for Lughnasad, Lugh, for Samhain, Lord Samhain himself, and so on. She had a feel for the indigenous deities of the landscape and her workings were not simply pretty yet empty words but experiences that actually changed you. The imagery was rich, deep and inspiring and there was no-one there going 'I am the great high priestess'. For me, this way of working was perfect.

As time went on, certain of us were drawn to the feline Egyptian deities, Bast and Sekhmet. Although we now do a lot of work researching these goddesses in a visionary sense, and performing rituals based around them, we still celebrate the eight seasonal festivals from a Celtic perspective, and also do other magical workings, involving other deities, when the occasion merits it. Our system is given in full in the forthcoming book, *Bast and Sekhmet: Eyes of Ra*, which I've written with Eloise Coquio.

As to how my magic relates to my work, all I can say is that my writing is part of my magic. I put my will and intention into it, so every novel and story is a kind of magical working. As I learn more, it goes into my fiction. When I wrote the Wraeththu books, I didn't describe the protagonist Pell's magical training in detail. I realise now this was because I knew so little of the subject back then. If I was writing that book now, no doubt the entire middle section would be about his magical apprenticeship, so it's probably a good thing I didn't know as much then!

I hope this has satisfied the curiosity of those who have asked me about my involvement with magic, but I'm happy to answer specific questions on this page if it hasn't.

When I produced the revised edition of 'The Enchantments of Flesh and Spirit' in 2003, I did in fact include more of Pellaz's magical training.

Blessed Are The Healers

Web Site Article on Reiki, 2000

Reiki is a form of healing that came to the West from Japan in the early 20ᵗʰ Century. I was intrigued by it when a friend suggested I learn it, but was not prepared for what I discovered once I started to research Reiki's history.

Before I actually learned about Reiki's background, I presumed the reasons people wanted it was either to work on their own self-development or else heal others. If I fell into either of those categories, then it was the former, although the main reason I decided to 'get' Reiki some time ago, was because my friend Paul Weston, whose opinion I greatly respect, suggested it for a different reason. As I was involved in a lot of visionary questing work at the time, he thought I'd find Reiki of benefit in keeping healthy in mind and body.

It was only once I had Reiki for myself and decided to delve into the subject that I discovered what I'd assumed to be a fairly newly-discovered and exciting form of energy healing was in fact the subject of heated factional battles within the Reiki community that had been going on for some time. Not only that. A great many people were making pots of money out of Reiki, and it was difficult for me to see any philanthropy and altruism in their vicious attempts to secure their source of income by discrediting rivals. What I had believed to be a wise, gentle body of loving healers turned out to be a snarling pack of adversarial wolves. An unpalatable truth struck me. Not everyone who acquired Reiki used it altruistically. As with so many things in our modern world, the desire for affluence was sometimes the prime motivating force.

Paul advised me to buy William Rand's book, *Reiki: The Healing Touch*, because – in his words – it was one of the most sensible. Rand had done a lot to debunk many of the popular myths about Reiki and its founder, Mikao Usui. Rand had learned that a lot of the so-called history of Reiki had actually been made up or embellished upon, perhaps to fit in with Western and/or Christian values. However, the truth was just as fascinating. Rand was also against exploitation, i.e. charging unfeasible amounts for initiation. I recommend any Reiki practitioners to read Rand's books, if they haven't already done so. From reading Rand, I bought books by Frank Arvata Petter, because I noticed Rand had written the introduction to one of them. I assumed that if he was happy to endorse Petter's book, it was probably OK. In fact, Petter's work greatly expanded my understanding and awareness of Reiki, and inspired me to be creative with it.

From the start, I had felt uncomfortable with the fact that Mrs Takata, who'd first brought Reiki to the West from Japan, had charged extortionate amounts of money for bestowing the third degree, Reiki Master. Her view was that people wouldn't appreciate Reiki unless they had to pay a lot for it. Its high cost was an indication of how precious it was. Although, with the greatest benefit of the doubt, you can perceive *some* justification for this, I cannot condone the fact that Reiki Master was then only available to the more affluent members of society. Just because you can afford $10,000 to become a Reiki Master doesn't make you more suited to acquiring it than someone who'd have a hard time getting $100 dollars together.

Fortunately, some Reiki Masters felt the same and the price for all three degrees of Reiki plummeted drastically, which allowed it to become more popular and easy to acquire. When I first became a Reiki Master, I considered that I would never charge anyone for attunements, but given the enthusiasm with which my friends flocked to my door, I realised there has to be a cut-off point. It's all very well initiating your best mates and family for free, but when a friend of a friend's boss's mother comes along, you realise you either have to make a nominal charge or refuse to oblige them. As a self-employed writer, my time literally is money. I couldn't spend all day, every day giving Reiki and not have time for anything else. I realised that if I initiated those closest to me for free, and they went on to become Reiki Masters, they could then initiate a certain number of people without charge, and so on. This would help spread the healing power of Reiki without exhausting me, or taking up all my time. I do think it's important that people are given the opportunity to have this gift for themselves, whoever they are and whatever their circumstances, which is why I'm so against high charges.

Another thing I'm against is dogma, and some of the information I've seen about Reiki certainly amounts to this. Frank Petter faced all kinds of problems because of his views, which were seen by the Reiki 'establishment' as virtually heretical. My reading informed me that rancour, spite and bitterness flew around wildly between various 'schools' of Reiki. When I first discovered this, I was extremely disappointed. Surely, the whole point of Reiki coming to the Western world was to help heal ourselves and our environment, to make people more aware and spiritual? There is little evidence of this in the petty in-fighting that occurs between some Reiki schools. For some reason, certain Masters feel theirs is the only 'proper' Reiki: a view with which I heartily disagree. Reiki is a dynamic system that constantly changes. Symbols and methods might mutate, but if the energy behind them is constant, how can it matter?

When I was given Reiki II and Reiki Master by Paul, he stressed how the symbols were secret, and not supposed to be written down. The initiate should learn them by heart. However, he allowed me to make copies of them, provided I'd keep them away from uninitiated eyes. His reason for the secrecy was that when someone receives second degree initiation, and they see the symbols for the first time, they have a greater impact on the subconscious than if the symbols were already familiar and known. The symbols 'do not work' without second degree attunement, so what's the point of knowing them beforehand anyway? He told me that some writers had broken this rule and had published the symbols, and I'd read in certain Reiki manuals about this, which was viewed rather dimly by the writers concerned.

I acquired Diane Stein's book, *Essential Reiki*, precisely because she'd published the symbols. In the book, the author states that Reiki is changing so rapidly, with so many new schools popping up, that there's a danger of the original symbols being lost, or at least they won't be known by initiates coming from non-traditional schools. She justifies publishing the symbols just for the record, so to speak, and I can't argue with that. I was intrigued to see just how much the symbols Paul had given me differed to those Ms Stein had received. Mine were listed as 'alternate' versions, (obviously the author will give hers as the main ones, because these are the ones she learned from her own Masters – in her position, I'd do the same), but she points out that Mrs Takata herself often changed the symbols during initiations, so there must be quite a lot of variants out there. The book is really a manual for Reiki Masters, but because it will sit next to more elementary works on book shop shelves, inevitably people with only Reiki I, or even just interested people, who have yet to acquire Reiki, will buy it. This is unavoidable, and not the most desirable circumstance, but I still support Ms Stein's position. Reiki's progress should be documented, and it's very useful for new Reiki Masters to have access to this kind of material. Not everyone wants to join an association or attend organised Reiki events.

Another thing I find difficult to condone is that most Reiki Masters (who advertise) offer only workshops and courses, during which a group of people will be attuned. I personally would not have liked to be given Reiki in a group workshop situation with a lot of other people I didn't know. Attunement can affect people in powerful ways, and sometimes students might become emotional, and wish to speak of issues that are private and personal. Paul always gives Reiki attunements on a one-to-one basis, and this is something that I elected to make my practice as well. Attunement ceremonies should be special, personal events, and take as long as is necessary. In a group situation, one person might need more support and comfort than others, which could result in people whose attunements were quite a smooth ride not getting as much support or opportunity for discussion. Also, should someone have a severe reaction, (which admittedly is rare), they might feel intimidated by the presence of strangers, even to the extent of bottling up their feelings and not expressing them. During attunement, the ideas is to release repressed feelings, to purge yourself of past 'baggage', so it's important students feel completely comfortable with 'opening up'. Even if you're not affected emotionally too much, information about your spiritual path in life can crop up through visualised images, and I believe a committed Reiki Master should then expand upon those messages, spending as much time with the student on it as required, which again might not always be possible in a group situation with limited time. Paul and I did several meditations during my initiations, on imagery that came to me during the attunements.

The more I learn about the Reiki 'community', the more it seems to me that too many people are into it to make money out of others. Fortunately, through teachers like William Rand, much has been done to bring down the price of attunement, but it seems as if the financially motivated have found a way round this. There are now many different 'brands' of healing, which have derived from Reiki, but which incorporate new symbols and techniques. As with Reiki in the Eighties, these systems are expensive to learn, a situation that maintains the exclusivity of certain healing methods. I will never agree with the justification that paying these high costs demonstrates a kind of respect for the healing energy, and that if someone goes to the trouble of investing that kind of money, they won't take the initiation lightly. This, to me, is utter arrogance on behalf of the so-called Masters. Of course, I want anyone I attune to Reiki to use it and benefit from it, but it really isn't my business what they do with it once they leave my house. The fact is that Reiki is theirs for life, whether they practice diligently every day, heal the whole world, or else slowly forget about it and go on to another fad. I wouldn't like people taking attunements lightly, but it's really not my concern if they do. Reiki power isn't mine; I am simply a channel for it. I can't make judgements on those who receive it. I'm privileged to be able to pass it on, and if in some small way it makes the world a better place, that's enough.

I've read of individuals wanting to trademark certain terms associated with all these techniques, in order to prevent others writing books or running courses on them. It flabbergasts me, because surely it's against all that Reiki and its derivatives stand for. Why is it that this fabulous gift comes into the world, only to be abused and exploited for gain? Reiki changed my life in a positive way, and I can't understand how people can just view it cold-heartedly as a lucrative business venture. I don't mean to imply I'm against people earning a living from Reiki, because only a fool wouldn't appreciate there are marvellous healers and teachers out there, who really should be devoting their entire lives to their vocation – and everyone has to eat! What I am against is elitism and greed. Just as I have issues with certain Eastern gurus who have very comfortable lifestyles indeed, thanks to the donations of their devotees, I don't think it's right to over-charge. There will always be desperate people willing to pay anything to make sense of their lives, to feel better, to feel whole. The unscrupulous can take advantage of that.

Reiki fascinates me, and has become a way of life, and I would love to know more about the modern derivatives, and see where creative and inspired people have taken it. But I refuse to pay through the nose for the privilege.

Reiki's Fire

Web Site Article, March 2002

I am not a New Age ascetic. I smoke, I drink, I eat meat, I have sugar in my tea and salt on my spuds. I do not meditate for hours a day and find it very difficult to believe the universe loves me. Therefore, it might seem odd that I have become a 'Master' (is there such a thing?) in a system that seems the very essence of New Age practice. The fact is that Reiki works for anyone, regardless of their spiritual beliefs and the way they live their life.

I first heard about it from Paul Weston, a friend who was already a Master. He suggested that because at the time I was involved in some intensive magical work, I should take First Degree Reiki initiation, as this would help ground me, and maintain healthy levels of energy. I was not immediately taken with the idea, believing Reiki to be some 'eastern thing' that Paul had got into. Pictures of gurus adorned his walls, and that wasn't really my 'bag'. All I knew was that Reiki was a kind of hands-on healing system, and I really couldn't imagine myself having the patience to sit there for hours on end with my hands on someone without getting bored. However, another friend of mine, who was going through a difficult time, took the plunge and went for First and Second Degree with Paul. The experience totally amazed her and she encouraged me to go for it as well.

I was attuned into the first two Degrees over the course of a long weekend in Glastonbury. I'd heard that once you were attuned to Reiki, you could really feel it coming out of your hands. I'd already learned that Reiki is 'chi', or universal life force, and that being attuned by a Master enables you to channel this energy through your own body. You can heal yourself with it, other people, animals and plants. Once you've taken Second Degree, and learn some of the Reiki symbols, you can 'send' Reiki over distances, into the future or the past. You can even send Reiki into a situation to help resolve it. Sounds like magic, yes?

On the way to Paul's, I tried to imagine what it might be like to be a universal life force channel, and just couldn't believe it could ever happen to me. I was not particularly psychic and certainly no healer. But my scepticism was utterly swept away. At the end of that weekend, I was so sensitive, I swear I could hear the grass grow, and *something* was blasting out of my hands like red hot laser beams. I was convinced. This was for real. The hyper-sensitivity didn't last, and after a good night's sleep, my feet were firmly back on the ground, but Reiki still poured out of my hands whenever I wanted it to.

Despite my passionate interest in all things esoteric, I'm naturally quite a sceptic, and at first I did wonder whether I could feel these effects simply because I *believed* I could. The human mind is a powerful thing and is quite adept at making things up, then experiencing them as pure reality. However, the fact that my cats not only reacted well to Reiki, but could also 'turn it on' in me without my even realising it was what finally assured me I wasn't just kidding myself. I was sitting watching TV one night, and my oldest cat, Tubbsy, (now 17), got onto my lap. (We have nine cats, who are all very friendly, and to be honest, when I'm lost in a movie I don't usually notice when one of them climbs onto me.) Then, I sort of came to my senses and realised I'd put my hands on Tubbsy and had been 'Reiki-ing' him for about half an hour. Usually, you turn Reiki on simply by intending it will happen, or visualising the symbols, if you know them. But when Tubbs wants Reiki, he doesn't wait for me to realise he's in need of bit of a blast. He simply finds the nearest practitioner, (and since I became a Master I've attuned many of my friends), gets on their lap and turns on their Reiki. His intention, not theirs! For an ancient cat, he is certainly very spry and healthy, and now looks younger than he did before I learned Reiki. That to me is the proof there's something in it.

Another thing that took me by surprise was that I didn't get bored during a healing. If anything, I just floated off into another realm, and could work creatively at the same time as giving someone a Reiki treatment. Once you're channelling Reiki, you don't have to think about it. It doesn't deplete or exhaust you to give a healing, because it isn't your energy. It comes from somewhere else. It has certainly had an effect on me, because I'm a much more positive person than I used to be, and far less prone to bouts of depression and stress. It isn't a miraculous 'cure all', but I feel it enables me to cope with life's ups and downs far more calmly and optimistically. I was so impressed by Reiki, I decided I wanted to be able to pass it on to others, so Paul kindly gave me Master Teacher training.

Some people would no doubt be put off the idea of Reiki by the dozens of books now available. Most of them come at it from a strictly New Age angle, and the message is often that in order to be a practitioner, you have to virtually live on soil and water, and be stringently ascetic. Many of these books are pious and patronising, and if I'd read them before I'd been attuned, I doubt I would ever have gone to Glastonbury for it at all. All I can say to this is that if that kind of lifestyle doesn't appeal to you, you can still be a Reiki practitioner, no better or worse than anyone else. Reiki bypasses the personality, if you like. Anyone can do it, regardless of how they live.

Attunement isn't an exam you either pass or fail. It's a very functional process, just like plugging an appliance into the mains. You are the appliance, Reiki is the power source and the Master/Teacher is the person who picks up the plug and fits it into the socket. As to how attunement actually works, nobody knows. There are now dozens of different ways to attune people, and they all work. What they have in common is the Reiki symbols and focused use of the breath.

If you take the Third Degree and become a Reiki Master, it does not mean that you suddenly become an enlightened super being. All it means is that you are taught the traditionally secret method of how to pass Reiki on to others. Teacher is probably a better word than Master, which does not mean the same in the West as it does in the East, where Reiki originated. Many books have now been published that reveal the symbols and the methods of attunement, but these won't work on their own. The ability has to be passed on through a Teacher. There are no doubt exceptions in the world: that is, people who can channel Reiki naturally, but for most of us, the traditional attunement is the only way.

I've met healers, who use colour energy or spiritual energy, and who have trained for many years in their system to become proficient. They have often been scathing of Reiki, because it takes so little time to learn it. First Degree can be taught in two sessions of a couple of hours each, during which four attunements are given. After that, the student can channel Reiki for life, and there is no need to take further Degrees unless they are interested enough to pursue their studies. How can something so powerful be learned so easily? I can understand why some people are suspicious of it. However, the fact is that Reiki can be learned quickly and easily. Some writers have suggested that the often high cost of attunement ensures it doesn't come *too* easily. I am completely opposed to such a viewpoint and teach Reiki at a reasonable price. What students pay for is my time, not the Reiki itself, which is free. How can I charge for something that isn't mine in the first place?

I firmly believe that First Degree Reiki should be everybody's birthright. It seems to me like a natural faculty that somehow we have lost and need to relearn.

Pyewacket, Grimalkin and the Sisters of Bubastis:
the Cat in Magic
Web Site Post, November 2004

The last few articles in this book comprise a series of pieces I wrote for a magical publication – either printed or web site; unfortunately I didn't keep a record of it! I then reproduced the articles on my own web site – a version of it that is now defunct. I was asked to contribute these pieces as I'd recently co-written a book on Egyptian cat and lioness goddesses. At this time, over ten years ago, Bast and Sekhmet, and other feline/leonine god-forms, were not widely known outside of pagan circles.

More than any other animal, domesticated or otherwise, the cat has always been associated with magic, mystery and the night. She is one of the essential symbols of the witch, the mysterious familiar who might, or might not, be something far more curious than a simple animal.

A cat chooses to spend her time with humans; she is not beholden to us. She is not by nature a pack animal, and is more than happy in her own company. It's intriguing to think about how this small bundle of sophisticated disdain decided that mere humans were worth hanging around with.

It's likely that cats noticed at one point in history that human settlements attracted vermin and therefore provided easy game. Also, humans had the useful skill of building fire, and cats love warmth. So how did the cat acquire her iconic status as a creature of magic?

Primarily, she is a creature of the night in its literal sense; she can walk softly, as if invisible, and her eyes glow like moonstones. Her cry of rage is like that of a banshee, and for an animal relatively so small she has the capability to inflict astonishing injury on the unsuspecting human. Orders to a cat are treated with contempt. She does not seek to curry favour as a dog does. If she gives you her companionship, you're always aware it's under her terms. It's likely that this lack of respect contributed to the view held by religiously-inclined people that the cat had an unsavoury alliance with dark forces. The cat is also a relative of far more dangerous felines, in particular the lion.

In Ancient Egypt especially, people believed that lions were magical because they lived in the desert; a place intrinsically inhospitable to life. The Ancient Egyptians are the people first credited with domesticating cats. The animal in question was a desert cat, with similar markings to a tabby, but with the lithe body of a breed like the Abyssinian. One of the most well-known, and currently best-loved, of Egyptian goddesses is cat-headed Bast, whose attributes included a love of perfume and dancing. However, the earliest Egyptian cat-featured deities had a purely leonine aspect, even Bast. The lioness goddesses were seen as aspects of the sun god, Ra, in particular his fiery wrath. Most of them were known as 'Eyes of Ra', and it was believed that Ra could send these implacable goddesses out to wreak havoc, especially when it involved smiting the enemies of the pharaoh. It was only in later times, when the Greeks had influenced Egyptian culture, that Bast became commonly associated with the domestic feline, and swapped her fierce lioness head for the more familiar cat face.

Bast was not regarded as a 'goddess of cats', but rather a goddess whose sacred animal was the cat. Her ancient aspect has been 'updated' by modern magical practitioners, so that she has now acquired different attributes to her earliest forms. Just as the Greeks gave her a lunar aspect, by associating her with their goddess Artemis, so modern magical practitioners have reinvented her to be pertinent to our times and requirements.

Whether the European view of the cat was influenced by her status in Egypt is open to question, but whatever the history, she has become synonymous with magic, and few modern witches are without at least one feline in their household. Many of them will tell you that their cats appear interested in ritual proceedings, usually by protesting loudly if they are excluded from a room where any magic is taking place. Of course, this might be more to do with the cat's contrary nature concerning areas off-limits to them, but from my own experience I can say that my cats do appear to enjoy being part of a magical circle, to the extent where their behaviour is more than coincidental.

Cats are associated with magical traditions in many other parts of the world, as well as Egypt and Europe. Pyewacket and Grimalkin are traditional European names for witches' familiars. And Bubastis was the city where Bast's biggest temple stood. But there are magical felines in legends of the Far East and Babylonia too.

Those of us who are drawn to magic: perhaps, when we gaze upon our feline companions, we should not attempt to penetrate their secrets, but rather take the chance to walk with them in the night, upon the lonely moonlit pathways, to discover what mysteries might be revealed.

Bast, Great Cat of the Heavens
Web Site Article, January 2005

Hear us, Bast the wonder worker.
Thou can twist the skein and entangle the thread of destiny.
Thou art Sekhmet-Bast-Ra, the sacred, the beautiful,
The lady of music, the lustrous, the all powerful.
The world rides upon the arch of thy back.
Thou art sacred.
Thou art venerated and called The Lady of the East.
Be favourable unto us.

From a litany to Bast by Elizabeth St George

My earliest memory of Bast is when, as a small child, I saw the Disney film *The Three Lives of Thomasina*. While this is a rather trite and not too brilliantly acted movie, there is one scene within it that stands out from all the rest. At the end of one of her lives, Thomasina, a ginger cat, goes to cat heaven. What she finds there is a staircase covered in cats and at the top of it an enormous statue in gold of a cat-headed woman: Bast, the feline goddess. This image had a huge impact on my young mind; it awed and inspired me. My first efforts at writing were little illustrated stories of Egyptian gods. A few years ago, I saw the film again, and it hasn't travelled too well, but still that one scene works brilliantly. I wonder how many others, who now regard themselves as priests and priestesses of Bast, were similarly inspired by it? That same film rather tentatively touches upon the concept of benign witchcraft too – interestingly enough. Quite radical for its time. Perhaps we should think about reclaiming it as one of the earliest media proponents of modern paganism!

In her original form in Ancient Egypt, Bast had a lioness's head rather than cat's. Along with the fearsome Sekhmet, and other leonine deities, (or neteru as they were properly called), she was an 'Eye of Ra'. These ferocious goddesses represented the heat of the desert sun, and were, when occasion merited it, sent out by Ra to smite his enemies. The Eyes of Ra were also called upon to deal mercilessly with any enemies of the reigning pharaoh.

It's a misunderstanding to think that the Ancient Egyptians worshipped thousands of different gods, or indeed revered idols of stone. The idea of neteru is one deity with many different faces or aspects, and the statues of these beings represented temporary vessels in which their essence, or heka, could reside in order to communicate with creatures of the Earth. The priests, as well as the musicians and dancers who worked in the temples, would 'persuade' a particular neter to enter their statue by making offerings they were thought to find pleasing, such as sumptuous food and drink, rare perfumes, as well as entertainment in the form of music and dancing.

The Egyptians did not have detailed 'histories' for all of the neteru. While the Greeks and Romans chronicled the exploits of their gods and goddesses in great detail, only a few Egyptian deities, such as Isis and Osiris, Shu and Tefnut, and Sekhmet, have such stories associated with them. It's also likely that the majority of these tales derive from the later period of Egyptian history, when other races had had an influence on the local belief system. No anecdotal material about Bast survives – if indeed it ever existed in the first place. We do know that she had sons – Mahes, Nefertum and Khonsu – but very little else. In some areas, she was regarded as the consort of the creator god, Ptah, as was lioness-headed Sekhmet. Both Mahes and Nefertum possessed lion-headed forms, while Khonsu was a lunar deity represented in human form.

Once the Greeks took power in Egypt, they equated Bast with their moon goddess, Artemis. In this way, Bast also acquired a lunar aspect. Her appearance changed, so that she took on the familiar head of a cat. The typical Egyptian statue of a seated cat does not characterise the goddess herself, but rather represents her sacred animal. However, for modern ritual purposes, when you might not have a statue of her in her cat-headed woman aspect, these cat statues make excellent substitutes to be placed on your altar.

The hieroglyph for Bast's name includes a symbol of a perfume jar, and it seems likely that perfume played an important part in her rites. She is a goddess associated with all kinds of sensual things: love, music, dancing and feasting. The Greek historian Herodotus visited Bubastis during one of the annual festivals to the goddess and left a very colourful account of the drunken behaviour of the celebrants. The festivals went on for days and were apparently quite orgiastic in nature. Nowadays, it's always appropriate, in any ritual to Bast, to include dancing and feasting as part of the proceedings. It's also pertinent to include anointing with perfume within the rite. Another of Bast's ritual 'tools' is the sacred rattle or sistrum. Most statues of her show her carrying one of these instruments. Although you can buy these fairly easily if you have access to the Internet, you can also make your own ritual rattle with dried seeds, beans or grains, which can be shaken in a jar or tub.

Although Bast is now regarded as a goddess of cats specifically, this was not the case in ancient times. The cat was her sacred animal, as most neteru had sacred creatures, but they would have been regarded as her messengers, or as earthly representations of her power. Cats were bred in Bast's temples, and there is a lot of evidence to show that this was mainly for the purpose of sacrifice. Nowadays, the thought of this is horrific to those of us who love cats and look upon Bast as a goddess associated with their welfare, but the Egyptians did not share our sentiments for domestic animals. If a cat was ritually killed, it was referred to as 'blessed', and could carry messages to the goddess in her heavenly realm. People would pay for this practice to be carried out, if they wished to communicate with Bast about their problems. Happily, such practices are no longer a part of working with this charismatic and intriguing goddess, and it's fair to say that the amount of belief, will and intention that has gone into reshaping Bast for modern times has evolved her into a bona fide patroness of feline creatures.

Most people who have worked with Bast will tell you that one thing she shares with her sacred animal is her nature. She is like a cat who will allow you to stroke her, and enjoy such contact, but she can also lash out with claws if you're not careful. There is a tendency in some pagan circles to 'water down' a lot of the ancient deities, to the point where they no longer have claws and are simply safe and fluffy shadows of their original forms. I cannot help but look upon this 'de-clawing' as a travesty. Bast is a powerful goddess, of conflicting but always fascinating aspects. She responds well to gifts, as any cat does. But just as with a cat, you should not take liberties with her. The most rewarding relationship you can have with Bast is one of mutual respect, tempered by both love and caution. She should, in my opinion, be allowed to keep her claws.

Sekhmet:
Lady of the Bright Red Linen
Web Site Article, April 2005

Like cat-headed Bast, Sekhmet is an 'Eye of Ra', in that she represents the solar power of Ra, the sun god. She was responsible for smiting the enemies of the pharaohs in ancient times. Her name means 'powerful' or 'violent', and it's likely that one of her many epithets, Lady of the Bright Red Linen, not only refers to the Red Land of the desert, where lions dwelled, but also to her bloodthirsty nature. She appears always as a lioness-headed woman, with a solar disk upon her head, wearing a long linen dress. She usually carries an ankh in her hand, symbol of life.

Sekhmet's main centres were in the south of the country, or Upper Egypt, whereas Bast's area was mainly the northern Delta area, Lower Egypt. The temples in the south are in better condition than those that stood in the more watery areas, so there is more information about Sekhmet than about Bast.

Many statues of Sekhmet have survived into modern times, and there is a wonderful array of them in the British Museum. It makes you cringe to consider it, but so many of these statues were shipped out of Egypt in Victorian times that they were sometimes used as ballast for the ships, thrown overboard in bad weather. There is a legend that one such statue lies at the bottom of the Thames. There's no doubt that Sekhmet has a definite presence in London. Not only are there the full-size seated and standing statues in the British Museum, but you'll find lion imagery all over the capital. You'll even find the head of one of the ancient statues above one of the auction houses in Bond Street.

While originally an extremely fierce goddess, among whose

attributes was the propensity to spread disease, Sekhmet has been reinvented by modern pagans and is now widely known and revered in pagan circles. Sekhmet still retains a vicious side, but her other aspects, as healer and self-empowerer have been brought to the fore.

Historically, she was a daughter of the sun, consort to Ptah, the creator god of Memphis and mother to the god Nefertum. Both Ptah and Nefertum were known for their great beauty, with the latter being specifically connected with the lotus flower. With them, Sekhmet made up the Memphite Triad. Although few anecdotal stories exist about the gods and goddesses of Egypt, there is quite a detailed one about Sekhmet. It concerns when Ra unleashed her upon humanity.

Ra had become displeased with the way humans treated him and felt that they needed to be taught a lesson. So he summoned his ferocious 'eye', Sekhmet, and ordered her to sort the humans out. Sekhmet was happy to oblige, but much to Ra's consternation, she didn't know when to stop. She delighted so much in the destruction and carnage, Ra feared that every last human would be killed. Realising he had released an uncontrollable force, he sought the help of his high priest at Heliopolis, who mixed beer with red ochre to create an intoxicating liquor that resembled blood. This, he scattered over the land. Sekhmet began to lap up the red beer, and drank so much of it she fell asleep. When she awoke, her bloodlust had gone.

It's said that before Sekhmet went on the rampage she was the gentle goddess Hathor, and only transformed into the fierce lioness once Ra had asked for her aid. Hathor and Sekhmet are closely connected.

The lioness goddess was also associated with the annual inundation of the Nile, albeit in rather a sinister way. The inundation marked the New Year in Egypt, and if for any reason it didn't occur, the country would die. Egyptians relied on the Nile to keep their narrow band of habitable terrain, the Black Land, fertile. And if the river flooded too much, it would be equally disastrous, as people, houses and farming land would be swept away. You can imagine that the days before the inundation were times of tension and anxiety. The heat was scorching, the river was low, and disease stalked the reed beds. The Egyptians believed this was the time when a seven-fold manifestation of Sekhmet walked among them, spreading famine and pestilence. These manifestations were known as the 'Slaughterers', and people did what they could to protect themselves in magical ways, such as tying pieces of red linen around their throats, which they believed would keep the Slaughterers at bay. Hathor also had a seven-fold aspect, but hers were seen as benign entities, who pronounced a person's fate at birth and could be petitioned in love and protection spells. Although Sekhmet's Slaughterers were seen to bring no good to humanity, the Egyptians had an interesting way of looking at it. They reasoned that if Sekhmet could cause disease, she must be equally proficient in healing it. In this way, she became known as a healer, and her priests were as much doctors as temple workers.

Interestingly, Sekhmet also had a male aspect. In this form she was ithyphallic and known as Sekhmet Min – clearly combined with the typically sexual imagery of the fertility god, Min. There is a wall relief depicting her in this way in the Temple of Khonsu at Karnak.

While it's obvious that in order to be pertinent today, Sekhmet's aspects needed to change and adapt, I do think it's important to remember her original form and what she represented. As with Bast, I've noticed a tendency for people to 'fluffy up' this magnificent goddess, to make her harmless and 'safe', which to me is a travesty. Many people who've worked with Sekhmet magically will tell you that it's not uncommon to feel her claws! She is a goddess to be treated with caution, in some respects, but is very rewarding to work with. She is far more likely to help you if you don't go before her on your knees. In my experience, she respects bravery and courage, and looks dimly on obsequiousness. She is ideal for help with self-empowerment, matters of justice and healing, and as a guardian or protector for the vulnerable. I have invoked her to protect a child in danger, for example, and also to help a little girl with leukaemia. One of the reasons she is such a formidable protector, especially for children, is because of her ferocity. Imagine how the lioness protects her young and you get the picture. A watered down, de-clawed version of her would not be as effective.

To sum up, I'd like to quote from the work of Elizabeth St George, from her booklet on Sekhmet, *Under Regulus*. This is part of a Sekhmet prayer, translated from the original Egyptian, and really makes the skin prickle:

> I am Sekhmet who cometh forth in the dawn.
> I am the power of Ra by day.
> I shall not be dragged back by my arms and none shall lay violent
> Hands upon me, lest I destroy them utterly.
> Neither man nor god shall hurt me, nor shall the living,
> Nor shall the holy dead detain me.
> Nor shall the demons destroy me in battle, for I am Sekhmet
> And I shall eat off their faces.
> I am she who cometh forth.
> I am yesterday and I am the seer of millions of years.
> I am the power of the divine judge. I dwell in the east.
> I am the lady of eternity, the unveiled one.
> My name is created to defy all evil.
> I am the flame that shineth in the sanctuary.
> I am Sekhmet.

The Lady of Moisture and the Lord of Slaughter:
More Leonine Deities from the Egyptian Belief System

Web Site Article, December 2005

The most well-known of Egyptian feline deities are of course cat-headed Bast and lioness-headed Sekhmet, both of whom have had a huge revival over the past decade as more and more people have been drawn to various pagan belief systems. But the Egyptians had thousands of gods and goddesses – known as neteru – and many of them had feline or leonine aspects. Some of them were little more than names or pictures upon the walls of tombs; neteru depicted in the Duat, or underworld. Others were more prominent. Among them were Tefnut, perhaps the first of all lioness goddesses, and Mahes, the lion-headed son of Bast.

Tefnut

Tefnut is a far older neter than Bast or Sekhmet, part of one of Egypt's creation myths that was devised by the priesthood in Heliopolis. The myth goes that Atum, the first neter of all, created Tefnut and her brother Shu on his own; that is, without a wife. Lioness-headed Tefnut was a goddess associated with moisture, even though lions were associated with the sun, and she was also known as an Eye of Fire, like Bast and Sekhmet. Her moisture is that of the sky, since Shu was regarded as a neter of the air. Moisture and air are of course needed to support life on this planet, so Tefnut and Shu were obviously symbols of these principles. The twins became lovers and

Tefnut eventually gave birth to two children: Nut, or Nuit, whose body is the starry sky, and Geb, who represents the earth itself. Like their parents before them, Nut and Geb became lovers, but this so enraged jealous Shu that he physically separated them; the air standing between earth and the heavens.

Nut was already pregnant when this separation was forced up her and her brother, but Shu cursed her so that she was unable to give birth on any day of the year. Nut however was resourceful and called upon the god Thoth, who was also one of her lovers. (We can only suppose that Atum had been busy making other children in the meantime!) Thoth gave to Nut five extra days that were outside the year. These are the epagomenal days that the Egyptians put into their calendar to keep things regular, much like we have to have a leap year every four years. On these days, Nut gave birth to Isis, Osiris, Set, Nephthys and, in some versions of the story, Horus the Elder. This family became known as the Ennead, which means comprising nine individuals, although if the older Horus is included this actually makes ten.

Of all the neteru, the Heliopolitan Ennead have the most stories surviving about them. The legends of Isis and Osiris and their siblings and children are fairly plentiful. Tefnut can be regarded as the mother of all neteru. In appearance she was very similar to Sekhmet, and in fact it's sometimes difficult to determine from statues which particular goddess you're looking at. She is depicted with a solar disk on her head and often carrying an ankh in one hand. Some sources say that while Sekhmet's ears tend to be rounded in artistic representations, Tefnut's are squared off. However, I'm not sure this is the case. For magical purposes, you could acquire a statue of Sekhmet and consecrate it to represent Tefnut instead, since it's unlikely you'll easily find a statue from any magical supplier that specifically represents Tefnut. As to her attributes, as well as being a goddess of moisture and gentle winds, she was said to represent the setting sun. Along with Shu, she comprised the Aker lions, the lions of yesterday and today. Shu represented the rising sun and Tefnut the setting sun. It's thought that the Great Sphinx, which faces east, is a representation of Shu, and that at some time there was a western facing twin sphinx that represented Tefnut. If it existed at all, this second sphinx has been lost to the sands of Giza, but the idea is an elegant one and makes sense. It would be nice to think that somewhere beneath the sand the sphinx of Tefnut lies sleeping.

Even though she is a goddess associated with water and the evening, Tefnut can't be regarded as a lunar deity. She is the mistress of the setting sun, the guardian of the dark hours, when the boat of the sun god sails through the Duat, (the Egyptian underworld), and she is the lady of the primal waters. Therefore, from a magical perspective, she can be approached as a goddess of learning and wisdom, since she is the first of all.

Mahes

Mahes is another neter who is currently enjoying a revival in pagan circles. He was credited as being one of the sons of Bast, along with Nefertum. His father was the sun god, Ra. Mahes was lion-headed, and his main cult centre was at Leontopolis, which recently has been subject to excavations. This means that more has been revealed about his cult. Mahes was a fierce neter who would attack the enemies of the pharaoh but he was also a god of healing – attributes that he shared with Sekhmet. Sometimes he was depicted as being a lion mauling a captive man. His consort was said to be Tekhait, a blood-drinking serpent goddess of fire.

It has been said that if someone wished to be initiated into the cult of Mahes they must undergo a process known as 'overcoming the lion', a procedure that was also known as the 'little death'. This initiation involved some kind of trial as the initiate had to overcome their worst fears and weaknesses in order to progress. It's also been suggested that the initiatory experience involved injury to and renewal of the left eye, which is known as the *mahit*, the eye that is associated with lunar and magical powers. Through this process the initiate acquired spiritual vision, so that they could see beyond the mundane world. The priests of Mahes were said to be able to see the spirits of the dead, and they did not fear death, because they believed they would be carried to the afterlife upon the shoulders of the god. Like his mother's, the rites of Mahes were supposed to have been celebrated with processions, music, dancing, and orgies.

Another legend associated with Mahes is that his priesthood would take offerings of milk and honey to rock caves high in the cliffs around his temples. Perhaps these offerings were to be devoured by the wild lions that lived in the desert. It's also been suggested that human sacrifice took place in the name of Mahes, and that the hearts of these victims were fed to the sacred lions that lived within the temples. The recent excavations have certainly revealed that lions were indeed bred and kept in these places.

As so little concrete evidence remains, all of these stories might simply be conjecture.

In terms of magical practice, Mahes guards the door to the astral plane, and his eye and hand guard the gates of night. He has many epithets, among them: 'Wielder of the Knife' (when he was represented as a phallic god); 'Lord of the Land of the Daughters' (a region of the afterlife); 'The Scarlet Lord' (perhaps a reference to the blood sacrifices carried out in his name); 'Helper of the Wise Ones', 'Lord of Slaughter', 'Manifester of Will', 'The Initiator', and 'The Avenger of Wrongs'. You can approach him magically to repel evil and to provide protection. He can also be invoked to stand guard during magical rites. He can be regarded as a god of the sense of sight and can be invoked to bring forth spirits for the purpose of divination or to find out the truth of a matter.

About the Author

Storm is the creator of the Wraeththu Mythos, the first trilogy of which was published in the 1980s. However, the influences and inspirations for the Wraeththu world go much further back than that, and continue into the future as she plans more stories for it.

Her other full length works cross genres from science fiction, to dark fantasy, to epic fantasy, to slipstream. She has written over thirty books, including full length novels, novellas, short story collections and non-fiction titles.

Storm is the founder of Immanion Press, created initially to publish her out-of-print back catalogue, but which evolved into the thriving venture it is today. Her interests include magic and spirituality, Reiki, movies, music and MMOs. Among her many occupations, most of which are unpaid, she runs a Reiki school and a guild called Equilibrium on the EU servers of World of Warcraft. She lives in the Midlands of the UK, with her husband and four cats.

Web site: http://www.stormconstantine.co.uk
Blog: https://dreamsofdarkangels.wordpress.com/

Also Published by Immanion Press

http/www.immanion-press.com

Wraeththu Mythos

The Moonshawl

A Wraeththu Mythos Novel

VII

THE CHARIOT

XI

JUSTICE

Storm Constantine

ISBN: 978-1-907737-62-6 £12.99

Published by Megalithica Books
an Imprint of Immanion Press

ISBN: 978-1-905713-13-4 £12.99

An imprint of NewCon Press

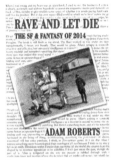

Rave and Let Die: The SF and Fantasy of 2014 by Adam Roberts
Award-winning author Adam Roberts makes no concessions when appraising the work of others. In this volume, he takes on the daunting task of providing an overview of the science fiction and fantasy produced during 2014. Featuring nearly 100 reviews, this book is packed with insight, wit, and honesty. Available as an A5 paperback (272 pages) ISBN: 978-1-907069-80-2 Price: £14.99

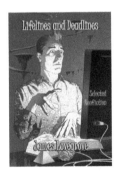

Lifelines and Deadlines: Selected Nonfiction by James Lovegrove
The articles and reviews of best-selling author James Lovegrove have appeared in print and online, including a regular review column for the *Financial Times*. Never timid, often contentious, sometimes amusing, ever insightful, always entertaining, *Lifelines and Deadlines* features the author's selection of his very best nonfiction from the past twenty years. Available as an A5 paperback (272 pages)
ISBN: 978-1-9010935-00-2 Price: £14.99

http://www.newconpress.co.uk